# THINK
# WELL ON'T

REFLECTIONS ON THE GREAT
TRUTHS OF THE CHRISTIAN
RELIGION, FOR EVERYDAY OF THE
MONTH

BISHOP CHALLONER

SENSUS FIDELIUM PRESS

Gastonia, North Carolina

# INTRODUCTION

I. Make choice of a proper time and place for recollection; and shut the door of thy heart as much as possible against the world with all its distracting cares and affections.

II. Place thyself in the presence of thy God, representing his incomprehensible Majesty to thyself by a lively faith, as filling heaven and earth, or as residing with all his attributes in the very centre of thy soul. Prostrate thyself in spirit before him, to adore this sovereign Lord; make an entire offering of thyself to him, humbly begging his pardon for all thy past treasons against him.

III. Implore, with fervor and humility, his light and grace, that the great truths of the gospel may make a deep impression on thy soul, that thou mayest effectually learn to fear and love him.

IV. Read the chapter for the day leisurely, and with serious attention, giving thy soul time to digest what thou art reading; and pause more particularly on those points which affect thee most.

V.That thy reading may partake the more of the nature of mental prayer, endeavor to draw from thy considerations such affections as arc suitable to the subject, by exciting for example in thy soul the fear and love of God; a confidence in his goodness; a sense of gratitude for his benefits; a horror of sin; a sincere repentance for thy past sins, etc, etc., open thy heart as much as possible to these affections, that so these great and necessary virtues may take the deeper root in thy soul.

VI. Conclude thy considerations with firm resolutions of amendment of life, insisting in particular on these failings to which thou art most subject; and firmly determining within thyself to put these resolutions in execution, upon such occasions as may occur that very day. VII. Reflect frequently in the course of the day on the chief points of the subject of thy consideration; lest the enemy rob thy soul of this divine seed, by making thee quickly forget what thou hast been reading and considering.

# CONTENTS

# 1

— · —

## FIRST DAY

### ON THE NECESSITY OF CONSIDERATION

CONSIDER, first, those words of the prophet Jeremias, with desolation is the whole earth laid desolate, because there is no one who thinks in his heart, Jerem. xii. 11. and reflect how true it is, that the want of consideration on the great truths of Christianity, is the chief source of all our evils. Alas, the greatest part of mankind seldom or never think, either of their Erst beginning, or last end: they neither consider who brought them into this world, nor for what end; nor reflect on that eternity into which they are just about to step. Hence all their pursuits are earthly and temporal, as if they were only made for this life, or were always to dwell here. Death, Judgment, Heaven and Hell, make but little impression upon them, because they do not give them leisure to sink deep into their souls by the means of serious consideration. They run on with their eyes shut to the precipice of a miserable eternity, and then only begin to think, when they find themselves lodged in that place of wo, where their worm shall never die, and their fire shall never be quenched. Ah! my poor soul, be thou careful that this be not thy case!

CONSIDER, secondly, that we cannot be saved without knowing God, and loving him above all things. Now we can neither know, nor love him, as we ought, without the help of consideration. It is this which discovers to us the infinite perfections of this sovereign Being: his charming beauty; his eternal love, and all the benefits which he has bestowed upon us his most undeserving and ungrateful creatures. All which, alas, make no impression on us without serious consideration. All things about us, the heavens, the earth, and every creature therein, cease not to preach God unto us, and invite us to love him: but without consideration we are deaf to the voice of the whole creation; we are like those that have eyes, and see not; ears, and hear not. Ah the great and dreadful mischiefs that follow from the want of that true knowledge of God, which is the fruit of daily consideration! Is it not upon this account that the whole, world is overrun with wickedness; and that hell opens wide its tremendous jaws, devouring without end or number the unhappy children of Adam, because God is forgotten, because there is no knowledge of God upon earth. Osea iv. 1.

CONSIDER, thirdly, that in order to save our souls we must know ourselves, our own misery and corruption, that we may become more humble and diffident in ourselves: we must know our irregular inclinations and passions, that we may fight against them, and overcome them: we must study and watch over the motions of our own hearts, that we may not be surprised by sin, and sleep in death. And how can this all-necessary knowledge of ourselves, this science of the saints, be acquired without the help of daily consideration? Ah, how unhappy are they who know all things, and yet are strangers to themselves! Let us then daily pray with St. Augustine, Noverim te, noverini me; Lord, grant me the grace to know thee, Lord, grant me grace to know myself: and let us labor to acquire two most necessary sciences by frequent consideration.

CONSIDER, fourthly, that in order to nourish in our souls the wholesome fear of God, which is the beginning of true wisdom, and spur ourselves on in the way of virtue, we must also seriously reflect on the enormity of sin, and the hatred God bears unto it; on the dreadful effect of sin in the soul, on the multitude of our own sins in particular; on the vanity, misery, and deceitfulness of the world; on the comfort and happiness that attends a virtuous life; on the shortness of time, and the awful length of a miserable eternity; on the certainty and uncertainty of death; on the sentiments We should have when we come to die; and on the small number of the elect, etc; Ah Christians, let us not neglect this great means of salvation! It was the consideration of these truths that made so many saints; that has so often reclaimed, even the most abandoned sinners. Oh, what a profound lethargy must not that soul be immersed in, which is not roused at the thunder of those dreadful truths. Death, Judgment, Hell, Eternity.

CONSIDER, fifthly, the bitter but fruitless repentance of the damned, condemning their past folly, for having thought so little on those things on which they shall now think for an endless eternity. "Senseless wretches as we were I we had once time, when, by thinking upon this miserable eternity, we might have escaped it. Those endless joys of heaven were offered to us at a cheap rate when a little reflection might have put us in the way of securing ourselves the everlasting possession of them. But we would not think then; and now, alas, it is too late." O my soul, learn to be wise by their misfortune; reflect, in this thy day, on the things that appertain to thy eternal peace; think well on thy last end; meditate on the great truths of the Gospel: for thou must either think of them now, or hereafter, when the thought of them will only serve to aggravate thy misery for all eternity.

# 2

## SECOND DAY

### ON THE END OF OUR CREATION

CONSIDER, *first*, O Christian soul, that so many years ago thou wast not yet come into the world, and that thy being was a mere nothing. The world has lasted near six thousand years, with innumerable transactions and revolutions in every nation, and where wast thou all that while? Alas, thou wast ingulfed in the deep abyss of nothing, infinitely beneath the condition of the meanest creature: and what couldst thou do in such a state? Learn then to humble thyself, whatever advantages thou mayest enjoy of nature or grace, since of thyself thou art nothing; and all that thou hast above nothing has been given or lent thee by thy Maker. Ah, poor wretch, what hast thou to be proud of? or what canst thou call My own, but nothing, and sin, which is worse than nothing.

CONSIDER, *secondly*, that the almighty hand of God, descending into the deep abyss of nothing, has drawn thee forth from thence, and given thee the being thou now enjoyest, the most accomplished and perfect of any in this visible world; capable of knowing and loving God in this life, and designed for the enjoyment of everlasting happiness with him in the next. Admire and adore the bounty of thy God, who, from all eternity, has designed this being for thee, preferable to so many millions of others which he has left behind, that had as fair a title to a being as thou hadst. Look forward into that immense eternity for which thou hast been created, and thankfully acknowledge, that the love thy God bears thee has neither beginning nor end but reaches from eternity to eternity.

CONSIDER, *thirdly*, that being created by Almighty God, and having received thy whole being from him, thou by the justice of all titles belongest to him; and art obliged to consecrate to his service all thy powers, faculties, and senses; and art guilty of a most crying injustice, as often as thou abusest any part of thy being, by employing it in the pursuit of vanity and sin. Ah! my poor soul, how little have we hitherto thought of this? How small a part of our thoughts, words, and deeds, has been referred to him who is our first beginning, and therefore ought to be the last end of all our actions? Be confounded at so great an abuse;—repent and amend.

CONSIDER, *fourthly*, that God who gave thee thy being, and who created all things else in this visible world for thy service, has created thee for himself alone. Not that he stood in need of thee, or can receive from thee any increase or addition to his happiness, but that he might give thee his grace in this life, and the endless joys of his kingdom in the next. Stand astonished, O Christian soul, at the bounty of thy Creator, in making thee for so noble an end! and since thou wort made for God, be ashamed to content thyself with anything less than God: learn then to contemn all that is earthly and temporal, as things beneath thee, and unworthy of thy affection. Lament thy past folly, and that of the greatest part of mankind, who spend their days in vain amusements and restless cares, about painted toys and mere trifles; seldom or never thinking of that great end, for which alone they came into this world.

CONSIDER, *fifthly* that all the powers and faculties of thy soul, viz, thy will, thy memory, thy understandings and all the senses and parts of thy body, were given by thy Creator, as so many means to attain this end of thy creation, to be employed during thy short abode in this transitory life, in the service of thy God, and so to bring thee to the eternal enjoyment of him in the sweet repose of his blessed kingdom. Alas, my soul, have we not perverted all these gifts of our Maker, in turning them all against the Giver. Have mercy upon us, O Lord, have mercy upon us; pardon our past treasons, and give us grace to begin now to be wise for eternity.

# 3

## THIRD DAY

### ON THE BENEFITS OF GOD

CONSIDER, *first*, my soul, how many and great are thy obligations to the bounty of thy God. He has thought of thee from all eternity; he has loved thee from all eternity: all the blessings and favors, which he has bestowed upon thee in time, he designed for thee from all eternity; they are all the consequences of his eternal love for thee. Is it possible that so great a God, the most High and the most Holy, who dwells in eternity, should set his affections upon such a poor sinful worm of the earth? Is it possible, my soul, that thou shouldst have had a place from all eternity in the heart of thy God; and that this eternal mind should never have been one moment without thinking on thee? Ah, poor wretch, what return hast thou made for this ancient love? How late hast thou loved him, who has loved thee from all eternity? How little hast thou thought of him, who always thinks on thee?

CONSIDER, *secondly*, that thy God has not only given thee by creation thy soul and body, with all their powers and faculties, and, in a word, whatever thou hast, and whatever thou art; but also preserves them each moment by the benefit of conservation, which may be called a continual creation. For as nothing but his almighty hand could give thee this being, so none but he could preserve thee from falling back into thy original nothing, which must infallibly have been thy case, if thy God had but for one moment withdrawn his supporting hand. Poor sinner, why didst thou not think of this when by thy repeated crimes thou wast waging war with thy God; and he with incomparable love was night and day watching over thee? How didst thou dare presume so often and for so long a time to provoke him, who held the thread of thy life in his hand, and who every moment could have crushed thee into nothing or cast thee headlong into hell! O, blessed forever by all creatures be his mercy, for having borne with thee so long.

CONSIDER, *thirdly*, the inestimable benefit of our redemption, by which our loving God has rescued us from sin, and from hell, the just reward of sin. Alas, my poor soul, we must have been lost forever, had not this sovereign Lord and Maker of heaven and earth loved us to that degree as to deliver himself up to the most cruel and ignominious death of the cross for our redemption. Greater love than this no man hath, that one lay down his life for his friend, St. John xv. 13. But, O dear Lord, thou hast carried thy love much farther, in dying for those, who by sin were thy declared enemies: in dying for such ungrateful wretches, as would scarce ever thank thee for thy love; and seldom or never so much as pity or take any notice of thy sufferings! Ah Christian, which shall we most admire, this great Monarch of heaven and earth (in comparison with whom the whole creation is just nothing, or rather less than nothing) expiring on a cross for such despicable worms as we are? or those, who believe this amazing truth, yet take so little notice of such immense love, which must be a just subject of astonishment to men and angels for all eternity.

CONSIDER, *fourthly*, how much we are indebted to God for having called us to the true faith, preferable to so many millions, whom he has left behind in darkness and- the shades of death. Alas, poor souls, how deplorable is their condition, void as they are of the knowledge of Jesus Christ, or of his only spouse, the true Catholic Church! flow little do they think of God, or of the life to come! With how little apprehension or remorse do they run on from sin to sin, and die impenitent: ah, the goodness of God, that has not suffered us to fall into such misery, though born and bred up amidst a people seduced by error or, if we have also had the misfortune, like our neighbors, to have gone astray from the womb, has by a more distinguishing mercy drawn us out of the dragon's jaws, and brought us to his fold, the Catholic Church! Blessed be our God for ever for all his mercies. O what an inestimable happiness it is to have, by the means of this grace of vocation, God himself for our Father, and his holy Church for our Mother! To pass this transitory life in the happy society of the only Spouse of God's only Son! to be daily partakers of the sacraments, those heavenly conduits of divine grace! to live and die in the communion of the saints, etc. Ah! Blessed is the people who have the Lord for their God. Ps. cxliii.

CONSIDER, *fifthly*, Christian soul, whoever thou art, the providence of God towards thee! With how many graces he has prevented thee from thy tender years: from how many misfortunes he has preserved thee. Has he not borne with thee for a long time, whilst others have been cut off in their sins? Are there not millions now burning in hell for lesser sins than thou hast committed? Reflect on the advantages thou hast received above thousands: what conveniences of life, what friends, what health, etc. while so many more worthy than thyself have been abandoned to want and misery. Ah, admire the unspeakable goodness of thy God to thee be astonished and confounded at thy past ingratitude: resolve from henceforth never to cease giving him thanks, and blessing his holy name.

# 4

## FOURTH DAY

## ON THE DIGNITY AND OBLIGATIONS OF A CHRISTIAN

CONSIDER, *first*, that every Christian by nature, and inasmuch as he is a man, is the most perfect of all visible creatures, endowed with understanding and reason; composed of a body whose structure is admirable, and of a spiritual and immortal soul, created to the image and likeness of God, and capable of the eternal enjoyment of him; enriched with a free will, and advanced by his Creator to the dignity of lord and master of all other creatures; though not designed to meet with his happiness in any of them, but in the Creator alone. Ah my soul, hast thou hitherto been sensible of the dignity of thy nature? Hast thou not too often, like brute beasts, looked no farther than this earth, viz. present, material, and sensible things? Hast thou not too often made thyself a slave to creatures, which were only made to serve thee?

CONSIDER, *secondly*, that every Christian, by grace, and inasmuch as lie is a Christian, has been by the sacrament of baptism advanced to the participation of the divine nature,

made the adopted child of God, heir of God, and co-heir
with Christ. He has been made the temple of the most High,
consecrated by the sprinkling of the blood of Christ, and
the unction of his grace; and received at the same time an
unquestionable right and title to an everlasting kingdom.
O Christian soul, hast thou ever yet entertained a serious
thought of the greatness of the dignity to which thou hast
been raised at baptism? How has thy life corresponded with
this dignity? O child of heaven, how long wilt thou be a slave
to the earth?

CONSIDER, *thirdly*, that as the dignity of a Christian
is very great, so also are the obligations that attend this
dignity greater than the generality of Christians imagine.
These obligations are briefly comprised in our baptismal
engagement. The first condition upon which we were
adopted into God's family by baptism, was that of faith.
The minister of Christ examined us at the font upon every
article of our belief; and to each interrogation we answered,
by the mouths of our godfathers and godmothers, Credo,
I do believe. What has thy faith been, O my soul? Has it
been conformable to this thy profession? Has it been firm,
without wavering? Has it been generous, so as not to be
ashamed of the doctrine of thy heavenly Master, or the
maxims of his gospel? Has it shewn itself in thy actions? or
hast thou not been of the number of those whose life gives
the lie to their faith? Of whom the apostle complains. Tit. i.
16. Who make profession of knowing God but deny him by
their works.

CONSIDER, *fourthly*, that at our baptism we made a solemn renunciation of the devil, and all his works, and all his pomps. Have we ever seriously reflected upon this renunciation? or do we rightly understand the obligations of it? And yet our title to the inheritance of our heavenly Father, is forfeited the moment we are false to this sacred engagement. Ah! my soul, if thou hast renounced Satan, take care that in the practice of thy life thou keep far from him: take care thou be no longer his slave by sin. Fly from all his works, the works of darkness: let him henceforth find nothing in thee that he may claim for his own, and by means of which he may also lay claim to thee. Despise his vain pomps, the false appearance of worldly grandeur, the prodigality, vanity, and sinful amusements by which he allures poor worldlings into his net: and if at any time thou art invited to take part in these fooleries, repeat to thyself those words of St. Augustine, What hast thou to do with the pomps of the devil, which thou hast renounced?

CONSIDER, *fifthly*, that at baptism each of us, according to the ancient ceremony of the Catholic Church, was clothed with a white garment, which the minister of Christ gave us with these words: Receive this white garment, which thou shaft carry without spot or stain before the judgment-seat of Christ. Happy souls, that comply with this obligation! What a comfort will it be to them in life! what a joy and satisfaction in death to have kept this robe of innocence undefiled! But, O baptismal innocence, where shall we find thee in this unhappy age? O blindness and stupidity of the children of Adam, that part so easily with so inestimable a treasure. Alas, my poor soul, has it not been thy misfortune? O make haste then to wash away, with penitential tears, those dreadful stains of sin, which must otherwise become the eternal fuel of hell's merciless flames.

# 5

## FIFTH DAY

### ON THE VANITY OF THE WORLD

CONSIDER, *first*, those words of the wisest of men, Eccles, i *Vanity of vanities, and all is vanity*: and reflect how truly vain are all those things which deluded worldlings pursue with so much eagerness: honors, riches, and worldly pleasures, are all but painted bubbles, which look at a distance as if they were something, but have nothing of real substance in them: and, instead of a solid content and joy, bring nothing with them but a trifling momentary satisfaction, followed by cares, uneasiness, apprehensions, and remorse. Ah bubbles indeed, which their admirers no sooner offer to grasp at, but they dissolve into air, and leave their hands empty! O how justly were all worldly enjoyments compared by the Royal Prophet to a dream? Dormierunt somnum suum, A nihil invenerunt omnes viri divitiarum in manibus suis, Psalm lxxv. They have slept out their short sleep, and when they awoke they found nothing in their hands of all those things, which in their dream they seemed to possess. *O ye sons of men how long will you be in love with vanity, and run after lies?* Psalm iv.

CONSIDER, *secondly*, that saying of St. Augustine, L. i. Confes. c. 1. Thou hast made us, O Lord, for thyself: and our hearts cannot rest till they rest in thee: and reflect, that our great Creator has given us a noble soul, made to his own image, and like, him spiritual and immortal, which therefore can never find its happiness in earthly and fading things. No, my soul, thou hast an understanding and a will capable of contemplating the sovereign beauty and sovereign truth, and of enjoying the one supreme infinite Good; and whatever is less than him, is not worthy of thee. Ah resolve then no longer to fatigue thyself, and waste away thy spirits in running like a child after butterflies: but since thou canst not be without seeking for happiness, seek it in the name of God where it is to be found, viz. in the way of virtue and devotion, and not in the by-paths which lead to endless misery.

CONSIDER, *thirdly*, the shortness of all worldly enjoyments. The days of man are very short: the longest life is less than a moment, when compared with eternity. *A thousand years, in the sight of God, the very truth, are but as yesterday that is past and gone*, Ps. Lxxxix. Alas! does not daily experience convince us, that we are here today, and gone tomorrow, and no sooner out of sight, but also out of mind? For as soon as we are in the grave, those that we leave behind think no more of us: *All flesh is grass*, says the prophet Isaiah, chap. x. and all the glory of it but like that of the flower of the field, which flourishes in the morning, and fades in the evening. *O how truly is our life* compared by St. James, chap, iv, *to a vapor or a thin smoke, which is dispersed by the first puff of wind, and no more seen? How justly is it* compared by Solomon, (Wisdom, chap, v.) *to a shadow, or to the flight of a bird upon the wing, or an arrow shot from the bow, which leaves no mark of its passage behind?* Ah! how vain then it is to fix our hearts upon what we must so shortly leave behind us.

CONSIDER, *fourthly*, what is now become of all the great ones of this world, those mighty monarchs, gallant generals, wise statesmen, celebrated beauties, etc. which made so conspicuous a figure a hundred years ago? Alas, they are all long gone; and now few or none ever think of them, or scarce know whether any such persons ever existed: just so it will be with us a few years hence. Ah worldlings, give ear for one moment to those who are gone before you; and who, from their silent monuments, where the remainder of their dust lies mingled with the common earth, call upon you in the words of the wise man: *Memento judicii mei; sic enim erit & tuum: mihi heri, tibi hodie*, Eccl. xxxviii. "Remember what we are come to; it will soon be the same with you: it was our turn yesterday; it will be yours today. We once, had, our parts to act upon the stage of the world; we once were young, strong and healthy, as you now are, and thought as little as you of what we are now come to: like you, we set our hearts upon trifles and toys, which we could but enjoy for a moment; and for these we neglected eternity. Senseless wretches as we were, we chose to be slaves to a cheating world, to inconstant perishable creatures, which abandoned us so soon, rather than serve that Lord and Master to whom nothing dies; and who neither in life nor death ever forsakes those who forsake not him." O Christians, let us take this warning; let the miscarriages of so many others teach us wisdom; let us not set our hearts on this miserable world, nor look upon anything as truly great, but what is eternal.

# 6

## SIXTH DAY

## ON THE HAPPINESS OF SERVING GOD

CONSIDER, *first,* those words of the prophet Isaiah, *Say to the just man, it is well,* Isai. iii. and reflect on the manifold advantages which this short word *well* comprises and ensures to the just, both for time and eternity. Honor, riches, and pleasure, are the things on which the world sets the greatest value: but they are not to be found where the world seeks them, but only in the service of God. Can any honor upon earth be comparable to that of being a servant, a friend, an adopted son of the great King of heaven? Such a soul is far more dignified in the eyes of God and his angels, than the greatest emperor in the universe. She is a child of the eternal Father, a spouse of the eternal Son, a temple of the eternal Spirit; heiress of the kingdom of heaven, and sister and companion to the angels. O my soul, let such honors as these be the only object of thy ambition.

CONSIDER, *secondly,* that the truest riches are to be found in the service of God; not indeed always those worldly possessions, which are attended with so many cares and fears, and daily exposed to so many accidents, and which are not capable of satisfying the heart; but the inestimable treasure of the grace of God, which is the seed of everlasting glory; the gifts of the Holy Ghost; the love of God; in a word, God himself, whom the world cannot take from the soul, unless she be so miserably blind as to force him away by mortal sin. Add to this, the fatherly providence of God, whose eyes are continually fixed upon the just, to watch over their welfare: that his angels always encamp about them to guard them by night and by day, Psalm xxxiii. 8. That as he formerly said to Abraham, Gen. xv. *He himself is their protector, and their reward exceeding great.* He is their friend, the best of friends; the shepherd of their souls, who leads them out to his admirable pastures, to the fountain of living water. His tenderness towards them is beyond that of a father, nay, beyond that of the tenderest mother, Isaiah xlix. 15, 16. In a word, God is all things to those that fear him. O my soul, seek no other treasure than him. Fear nothing but the losing him. If thou hast him, nothing can make thee miserable; but, without him, nothing can make thee happy.

CONSIDER, *thirdly,* the pleasure that attends a virtuous life; the satisfaction, peace, and joy of a good conscience, which by the wise man is compared to a continual banquet; the consolations of the Holy Ghost; the comfortable expectation of a happy eternity after our exit out of this vale of tears; a holy confidence in the protection and providence of God, and a perfect conformity in all things to his blessed will. From these fountains flow such delights, as cannot be conceived by worldlings who have no experience of them: pleasures pure and spiritual, which sweeten all the crosses of life, are an unspeakable comfort in death, and carry with them a certain foretaste of the immortal joys of heaven. Whereas all worldly pleasures, like the world itself, are false and delusive, always besprinkled with bitterness, attended by uneasiness, followed with remorse, and at last terminate in eternal sorrow.

CONSIDER, *fourthly,* the saying of our Savior, *one thing is necessary,* Luke x. 42. And what is that one thing, O my soul, which alone can make thee happy, both here and hereafter? It is to serve thy God; and to provide in earnest for eternity. As time, compared to eternity, is less than nothing; so are all temporal concerns, if compared with the concerns of eternity. This is thy only business: if thou art careful of this, all is well; but if thou neglect it, all is lost, and lost forever; As for all other things of which thou mayest stand in need in this life, give ear again to the same Savior, Matt. vi. 33. *Seek first the kingdom of God and his justice, tend all these things shall be given you over and above.* Conclude then, my soul, since both thy temporal and eternal welfare depends on serving God, to make this for the future thy only care. Thus only shalt thou meet true comfort here; thus only shalt thou come to never-ending happiness.

# 7

## SEVENTH DAY

### ON DEATH

CONSIDER, *first,* that there is nothing more certain than death. *It is appointed for all men once to die, and after that, judgment.* This sentence is general; it is pronounced on all the children of Adam: neither wealth, not strength, nor wisdom, nor all the power of this world can exempt anyone from this common doom. From the first moment of our birth, we hasten to death: every moment brings it nigher to us. The day will come, it will certainly come, and God only knows how soon, when we shall never see the night; or the night will come, when we shall never see the ensuing morning. The day will most certainly come, when thou, my soul, must bid a long farewell to this cheating world, and all thou hast adored therein; and even to thy own body, the individual companion of thy life; and take thy flight to another country, where all that thou settest a value upon here, will vanish like smoke: learn then to despise this miserable world, with all its enjoyments with which thou must part so soon, whether thou wilt or not.

CONSIDER, *secondly,* that as nothing is more certain and inevitable than death, so nothing is more uncertain than the time—the "place—the manner—and all other circumstances of our death. "O my soul," says St. Francis de Sales, "thou must one day part with this body: but when shall that day be? "Shall it be in winter, or in summer? in the city, or in the country? by day, or by night? Shall it be suddenly, or on notice given thee? Shalt thou have leisure to make thy confession? Shalt thou have the assistance of thy ghostly father?" Alas, of all this thou knowest nothing at all: only that it is certain thou must die; and that, as it almost always happens, thou must die much sooner than thou dost imagine.

CONSIDER, *thirdly,* that death being so certain, and the time and manner of it so uncertain, it would be no small comfort, if a man could die more than once, that so, if he had the misfortune once to die ill, he might repair the fault by being more careful a second time. But, alas, we can die but once: for when once we have set our foot within the gates of eternity, there is no returning back, if we die once well, it will be always well; but if once ill, it will be ill with us for all eternity. O, dreadful moment, on which depends an endless eternity! O blessed Lord, prepare us for that fatal hour.

CONSIDER, *fourthly,* the folly and stupidity of the greatest part of mankind, who though they daily see some or other of their friends, acquaintance, or neighbors carried off by death, and that very often suddenly in the vigor of youth, yet always imagine death to be at a distance from them: as if those arrows of death which are falling on all sides of them,

would not reach them too in their turn; or as if they had
a greater security than so many others who are daily swept
away. Senseless worldlings! Why will you not open your
eyes? why will you fondly imagine yourselves secure from
the stroke of death, when you cannot so much as promise
yourselves one single day of life? How many will die before
the end of this month, that are as young, as vigorous, and
as healthy as you are? and who knows but you may be of
that number? Ah, Christians, take care lest you be surprised.
Set your house in order: and for the future avoid sin, the
only evil which makes death terrible. Live always in those
dispositions in which you would gladly be found at the hour
of death. To act otherwise is to renounce both religion and
reason.

CONSIDER, *fifthly* the state and condition, of this
corruptible body of ours, as soon as we are dead: alas, it
immediately becomes pale, stiff, loathsome, and hideous;
insomuch, that our dearest friends can scarce endure to
watch one night in the same room with it, much less bear
to lie with it in the same bed; for so fast does it tend to
stench and corruption, that its nearest relations are the first
to wish it out of the house, and to lay it deep underground,
that it may not infect the air. But what companions, what
attendants must it there meet with? Worms and maggots.
For these, O man, thou art pampering thy body: these are
to be thine inheritance, O man! or rather they are to inherit
thee: whatever thou art today, tomorrow thou wilt be the
food of worms. Ah worldlings, that are enamored with
your own, or the beauty of others, and thereby too often

drawn from your allegiance to God, vouchsafe for once to reflect upon the condition to which both you and they must soon be reduced, and you will see what little reason you must fix your affections upon such painted dunghills, which quickly betray what they are, and end in noisomeness and corruption. We read that St. Francis Borgia was so affected with the bare sight of the ghastly countenance of the Empress Isabella after death, whom he had seen a little before in all her majesty and charms, as to conceive an eternal disgust of this world, and a happy resolution of consecrating himself wholly to the service of that King who never dies. Let the like consideration move us to the like resolution.

# 8

### — ı —

# Eighth Day

## ON THE SENTIMENTS WE SHALL
## HAVE AT THE HOUR OF DEATH

CONSIDER, *first,* Christian soul, what thy sentiments will
be at the hour of death with regard to this world, and all
its perishable goods, vain honours, false riches, and cheating
pleasures! Alas, the world must then end in thy regard; it
will turn upside down before thy eyes; and thou wilt begin
to see clearly the nothingness of all those things on which
thou hast here set thy heart. How wilt thou then despise all
worldly honours and preferments, when thou seest thyself
at the brink of the grave, where the worms will make no
distinction between the king and the beggar! How little
account wilt thou then make of the esteem of men, who
then will think no more of thee? How wilt thou undervalue
thy riches, which must now be left behind thee, when six
foot of land, a coffin and a shroud will be all thy possession?
How despicable will all worldly pleasures then seem to thee,
which at the best could never give thee any true satisfaction,
and which thou now beholdest to fly from thee, and dissolve
into smoke! Ah my poor soul, enter now into the same
sentiments which thou shalt certainly have at the hour of thy

death; as thus, and thus only, shalt thou be out of danger of being deceived by this deceitful world.

CONSIDER, *secondly,* what will then be thy thoughts with regard to thy sins; when the curtain, with which thy busy self-love has industriously hidden or disguised the deformity and malice of thy crimes, shall be withdrawn, and all thy sins shall be set before thy eyes in their true light: when so many things which thou wast willing to persuade thyself were but small faults, or none at all, will present themselves before thee in other kind of colours, as great and hideous offences: when that false conscience, which thou hast framed to thyself, and under the cover of which thou hast passed over many things in thy confessions, as slight and inconsiderable, which thou wast ashamed to declare, or unwilling to forsake, shall no longer be able to maintain itself at the approach of death. Ah what anguish, what confusion, what dreadful temptations of despair must such a sight as this give to the dying sinner? Learn thou, my soul, to take better measures now in time and thus to prevent so great a misery.

CONSIDER, *thirdly,* and take a nigher view of the lamentable state of a sinner at the hour of his death: when all things seem to conspire against him, and whichsoever way he looks for any case or comfort, he can find none. Before his eyes, he sees a whole army of sins mustered up: a viper's brood of his own offspring, which stick close to him, and assailing him with their united force, make him already begin to feel the gripes of that never-dying worm of conscience, which shall be the eternal torment of the damned. O how gladly would he shake off this troublesome company: but all

in vain; they are resolved not to leave him. If he looks back
into his past life, to seek for some good works to oppose this
army of sins; alas, he finds the good that he has done has been
so inconsiderable, so insignificant, as to give him no hopes
of its weighing down the scales, when balanced with his
multiplied crimes. His very prayers, and the confessions and
communions he has made, fly now in his face, and upbraid
him with his wretched negligence, and sacrilegious abuse of
these great means of salvation. The sight of all things about
him, his wife, his children, his friends, his worldly goods,
which he has loved more than God, serve for nothing now
but to increase his anguish. And what is his greatest misery
is, that the agonies of his sickness give him little or no leisure
or ability to apply himself seriously to the greatest and most
difficult of all concerns, which is, a perfect conversion to
God after a long habit of sin. O, how truly may, the sinner
now repeat those words of the Psalmist; *The sorrows of death
have encompassed me, and the perils of hell have found me.*
Psalm cxiv. O what unspeakable anguish must it be to see
himself just embarking upon eternity, an infinite and endless
duration, an immense ocean, to whose further shore the
poor sailor can never reach: and to have so much reason to
fear, it will be to him an eternity of wo.

CONSIDER, *fourthly,* my soul, what thy sentiments will
be at the hour of thy death, with delation to the service of
God, and to virtue and devotion: how lovely will the way
of virtue then appear to thee! How wilt thou their wish to
have followed that charming path! O what a satisfaction is
it to a dying man to have lived well! What a comfort to see

himself now at the end of all his labors and dangers; to find himself at the gates of eternal rest, of everlasting peace, after a long and doubtful war! He may now securely come down from his watch-tower, and repose himself for ever in the kingdom of his Father. O, what a pleasure, what a joy to look forward into that blessed eternity! O how *precious in the sight of God is the death of his saints,* Ps. cxv. Ah, *Let my soul die the death of the just, and let my end be like to theirs,* Numb, xxiii. Christians, if we would die the death of the just, we must live the life of the just! The only security for a good death, is a good life.

CONSIDER, *fifthly,* or rather conclude from the foregoing considerations on death, to make it the whole business of your life to prepare for death. Upon dying well depends nothing less than a happy eternity. If we die ill, we are lost, and lost for ever. As then, we came into the world for nothing else, but to provide for eternity, so we may truly say, we came into the world for nothing else, but to learn to die well. This is the great lesson which we must all study. Alas, if we miss it, when we are called to a trial, an endless duration of wo must be the necessary consequence. Ah, how hard is it to learn to perform that well, which can be done but once.

# 9

###### — · —

## NINTH DAY

## ON THE PARTICULAR JUDGMENT
## AFTER DEATH

CONSIDER, first, that the soul is no sooner parted from the body, but she is immediately presented before the judge, in order to give an account of her whole life, of all that she has thought, said, or done, during her abode in the body, and to receive sentence accordingly. For that the eternal doom of every soul is decided by a particular judgment immediately after death, we learn from the gospel in the example of Dives and Lazarus: and the sentence that passed here will be ratified in the general judgment at the last day. Christians, how stand your accounts with God? What could you be able to say for yourselves, if this night you should be cited to the bar? It may be perhaps your case. Remember that your Lord will come when you least expect him; take care then to be always ready.

CONSIDER, *secondly*, how exact, how rigorous his judgment will be, where even the least idle word cannot escape the scrutiny of the judge. O, what treasures of iniquity will here come to light, when the veil shall be removed, which hides at present the greatest part of our sins from the eyes of

the world, and even from our own: and the whole history of
our lives shall at once be exposed to our view. Good God!
who can be able to bear this dreadful sight? Here shall the
poor soul be brought to a most exact examination of all
that she has done, or left undone, in the whole time of her
pilgrimage in this mortal body: how she has corresponded
with the divine inspirations; what use she has made of God's
graces; what profit she has reaped from the sacraments which
she has received, from the word of God which she has heard
or read; what advantage she has made of those favorable
circumstances in which God Almighty has placed her; how
she has employed the talents with which he has entrusted
her: even her best works shall be nicely sifted: her prayers,
her fasts, her alms deeds; the intention with which she has
undertaken them; the manner in which she has performed
them: all these shall be weighed, not in the deceitful balance
of the judgment of men, but in the scales of the sanctuary.
Ah, how many of our actions will then be found to want
weight, according to that of Dan. v. Thou hast been weighed
in the balance, and art found of too little weight. O enter not
into judgment with thy servant, O Lord; for no man living
shall be justified in thy sight. Psalm cxlii.

CONSIDER, *thirdly*, the qualities of the judge before
whom we must appear. He is infinitely wise, and therefore
cannot be deceived; he is infinitely powerful, and therefore
cannot be resisted; he is infinitely just, and therefore will
render to everyone according to his works. No favor is to
be expected at this day: the time of merit and of acceptable
repentance is now at an end. Ah Christians, think well on't

now whilst it is your day: you may now wash away your sins
by penitential tears, and thus hide them from the eyes of
your future judge; you may at present tie up his hands by
humble prayer; you may appeal from his justice to the court
of his mercy, and cause him to cancel the sentence that stands
against you: but at that day you will find him inexorable:
your prayers and tears will then come too late.

CONSIDER, *fourthly*, the inestimable comfort that the
souls of the just shall receive at this day from the company
of their good works, which like an invincible rampart shall
surround them on all sides, and keep their hellish foes at a
distance. O my soul, let us take care to provide ourselves with
such attendants as these against that hour, which is to decide
our eternal doom. These are friends indeed, that will not
forsake us even in death; and will effectually plead our cause
at that bar where no other eloquence will be regarded.

CONSIDER, *fifthly*, in what a wretched plight the sinner,
who has taken no care to lay up any such provision of
good works, shall now stand before his judge. O how all
things now speak to him the melancholy sentence, that is
just now going to fall upon his guilty head. Whatever way
he looks, he sees nothing that can give him any comfort;
but on the contrary, all things that contribute to his greater
anguish and terror. Beneath his feet he sees hell open ready to
swallow him up: above his head an angry judge prepared to
thunder out against him the irrevocable sentence of eternal
damnation: on his right hand, he sees his guardian angel
now abandoning him; on his left the devils, his merciless
enemies, just ready to seize upon him, and only waiting

for the beck of the judge: if he looks behind, he discovers a cheating world, which now retires from him; if he looks before, he meets with nothing but a dismal eternity. Within he feels the intolerable stings of a guilty conscience: and on all sides he perceives an army of hideous monsters, his own sins, more terrible to him now than the furies of hell. Good God, deliver me from ever having any share in such a scene of misery.

CONSIDER, *sixthly*, that in order to prevent the judgment of God from falling heavy upon us after death, we must take care to judge and chastise ourselves, by doing serious penance in this life; for thus; and this only, shall we disarm the justice of God enkindled by our sins. Let us follow the advice of him who is to be our judge, who call upon us to watch and pray at all times; that so we may be found worthy to escape these dreadful dangers, and stand with confidence before the Son of Man. Luke xxi. 36. Ah, let this judgment be always before our eyes: let us daily meditate on this account that we are one day to give. Let us never forget that there is an eye above that sees all things; that there is an ear that hears all things; that there is a hand that writeth down all our thoughts, words, and deeds, in the great accounting book; and that all our actions pass from our hands to the hands of God; that what is done in time, passeth not away with time, but shall subsist after all time is past. O that men would be wise, and would understand these truths, and provide in earnest or their last end! Deuter. xxxii.

# 10

---·---

## TENTH DAY

## ON THE GREAT ACCOUNTING DAY

CONSIDER, *first,* that nothing can be conceived more
terrible than, the prospect which scripture gives us of the last
accounting day, with all the prodigies that shall go before it.
The sun darkened, the moon red as blood, the stars without
light, and seeming to fall from the firmament! the earth
shaken with violent earthquakes, the sea swelling and roaring
with unusual tempests, the elements all in confusion, and
whole nature in disorder. *The day of the Lord,* says the
prophet Joel, chap. ii. *a day of darkness and obscurity, a
day of clouds and whirlwinds. Before its face devouring fire,
and behind it burning fames. The earth shall tremble at the
appearance of it, and the heavens be moved at its sight. The
sun and moon are darkened, and the stars have withdrawn
all their light.* And the prophet Sophonias, chap. i. cries out.
*That day, a day of wrath, a day of tribulation and anguish, a
day of calamity and misery, a day of darkness and obscurity, a
day of mists and whirlwinds.* Can anything be more frightful
than these descriptions? Ah, what will then be the thoughts
of sinful many who sees himself threatened by all these signs.

Alas, he shall perfectly wither away with fear, in expectation of that tragedy which must follow these dreadful preludes.

CONSIDER, *secondly,* that the last day being come, fire raging like an impetuous torrent, shall, by the comand of God, consume the whole surface of the earth, and all that is thereon; nothing shall escape it. Where, O worldlings, will then be all your stately palaces, pleasant seats, gardens, fountains, and grottoes; where your gold, silver, and precious stones, etc. Alas, all that you set your hearts on in this world, shall in a moment be reduced to ashes; to show you the vanity of the things you loved, and your own folly in placing your affection upon such glittering shadows, upon such painted bubbles. Learn then, my soul, to despise this world, with all its goods, since all must end in smoke and ashes, and lay up to thyself treasures in heaven, which alone will be out of the reach of this last fire.

CONSIDER, *thirdly,* that the final end of this world being now come, the archangel shall sound the last trumpet, and raise his voice with a *Surgite mortui: Arise ye dead and come to judgment:* a voice, that shall at once be heard over all the universe, that shall pierce the highest heavens, and penetrate down to the lowest abyss of hell: at this voice, in an instant, by the almighty power of God, all the children of Adam, from the first to the last, shall arise from the dust, and each soul be united again to its respective body never more to be separated for eternity. O my soul, let this last trumpet always echo in thy ears! O take care to prevent the terrors of this summons, by hearkening now to another summons of the great trumpet of the Holy Ghost, who calls upon thee by the mouth of the apostle, *Arise thou that sleepeth, and rise from the dead,* that is, from the death of sin, *and Christ shall enlighten thee,* Eph. v. It is thus by having part in the first resurrection, thou shaft provide in time against that dreadful hour, when *time shall be no more,* Apoc. x. It is thus thou shaft escape the second death.

CONSIDER, *fourthly,* the wonderful difference there will be at the time of this general resurrection between the bodies of the just and the wicked. The just shall arise in immortal and impassable bodies, more pure, more beautiful than the stars, and more resplendent than the sun: but the wicked shall arise in bodies suitable to their deserts, foul, black, hideous, and in every other respect loathsome and insupportable; immortal, it is true, but to no other purpose, than to endure immortal torments. O what an inexpressible rack will it be to these wretched souls, to be reunited to such carcasses, to be condemned to eternal confinement in such horrid and filthy abodes! Ah my soul, take thou care to keep thy body now pure from the corruption of carnal sins, lest otherwise it become hereafter an aggravation of thy eternal misery.

CONSIDER, *fifthly,* with how much joy and satisfaction the souls of the just shall be again united to their bodies, which they have so long desired; with what affection they will embrace those fellow-partners in all their labors, sufferings, and mortifications; and now designed, to give an addition to their eternal happiness, by sharing in the glory of the heavenly Sion. But, O what dreadful curses shall pass at the melancholy meeting of the souls and bodies of the reprobate? Accursed carcass! will the soul say, was it to please and indulge thy brutish inclinations, that I have forfeited the immortal joys of heaven? Ah, wretch, to indulge thee in a filthy pleasure for a moment, I have damned both myself and thee to all eternity. O thrice accursed carrion! it is just, it is just, that thou, who hast been the cause of my damnation, shouldst be my partner in eternal wo. But oughtest thou not rather, unhappy soul, to be a thousand times more accursed by the body, since it was thy business, and in thy power to have subjected its passions and lusts to the rule of reason and religion; but thou didst rather chose, for the sake of a momentary satisfaction, to enslave thyself to its sensual inclinations, and so to purchase hell both for it and thyself. Ah Christians, let us learn to be wise by the consideration of the misfortunes of others.

# 11

## ELEVENTH DAY

## ON THE GENERAL JUDGMENT

CONSIDER, *first,* that immediately after the resurrection of the dead, all mankind shall be assembled together in the place designed for the last judgment, commonly believed to be the valley of Josaphat near Jerusalem, in sight of mounts Olivet and Calvary, where our Lord heretofore shed his blood for our redemption. O, what a sight will it be to behold all the children of Adam, that innumerable multitude of all nations, ages, and degrees, standing together, without any distinction as now, of rich and poor, great or little, master or servant, monarch or subject; excepting only the distinction of *good and bad,* which shall be wonderful and eternal. Alas, how mean a figure will an Alexander, a Caesar, or any of those great heroes of antiquity, whose very name has made whole nations tremble, then make? Those mighty monarchs, who had once the world at their beck, are now levelled with the meanest of their slaves, and would wish a thousand times never to have borne the scepter, nor worn the diadem.

CONSIDER, *secondly,* that the dead being now assembled together, the great Judge shall descend from heaven with great glory and majesty, environed with all his heavenly courtiers, and all the legions of angels. O how different from his first coming will this his second appearance be? His first coming was in great meekness and humility, because that was *our day,* in which he came to redeem us by his *mercy:* but at his second coming, it will be *his day,* when he shall arm himself with all the terrors of his *justice,* to revenge upon sinful man the cause of his injured mercy, with a final irrevocable vengeance. Miserable sinners! How will you be able to stand before his face, or endure his wrathful countenance? Ah, then it is you will begin to cry out to the mountains and rocks to fall upon you, and hide you from the wrath of the Lamb, from the face of him that sitteth on the throne. Nay, such a dread and terror will the very sight of the incensed judge carry with it, that you will even wish a thousand times to hide your guilty heads in the lowest abyss of hell, rather than endure this dreadful appearance: but all in vain, you must endure it.

CONSIDER, *thirdly,* that before the judge shall be borne the royal standard of the cross, shining brighter than the sun, to the great comfort of the good, and the unspeakable anguish and confusion of the wicked, for having made so little use of the inestimable benefit of their redemption. Here they shall see plainly how much their God has suffered for their salvation: how great has been his love for them, that boundless and unparalleled love, which brought him down from bis throne of glory, and nailed him to the cross. O,

how will they now condemn their obstinacy in sin, their
blindness and ingratitude! O, how will this glorious ensign
justify in the face of the whole universe the conduct of God,
and the eternity of hell's torments: for what less than a
miserable eternity can be sufficient punishment for so much
obstinacy in evil, after so much love?

CONSIDER, *fourthly,* how at the command of the
sovereign Judge, which shall be instantly obeyed, the
servants of God shall be selected from out of the midst of
that vast multitude, and placed with honor on his righthand;
whilst the wicked, with those evil spirits, whose parts they
have taken, shall be driven with ignominy to the left.
O, dreadful and eternal separation, after which these two
companies shall never more meet. And thou, my soul, where
dost thou expect to stand at that day? In which of these two
companies shalt thou be ranked? Thou hast it now in thy
choice: chose then now that *better part, which will never be
taken from thee. Fly now from the midst of Babylon;* renounce
now the false maxims, corrupt customs, and sinful pleasures
of worldlings; separate thyself from the wicked in time, that
thou mayest not be involved in their eternal damnation.

CONSIDER, *fifthly,* what will then be the thoughts of the
great ones of this world; what fury, envy, bitter anguish,
and confusion will then oppress their souls? When they
shall see the poor in spirit, the meek and humble, who
were so contemptible in their eyes whilst they were here in
this mortal life, now honored and exalted in the sight of
the universe; and themselves treated with such contempt?
Hearken to their complaints, as foretold by the wise man,

Wisd. v. *These are they whom heretofore we laughed at, and whom we made the subjects of our scoffs. Senseless* wretches *as we were, we esteemed their life madness, and their end without honor. See how they are now reckoned among the children of* God, *and with the saints is their* eternal *lot. Ergo erravimus a via veritatis.* Alas, after all, 'tis we are the people that have been mistaken; 'tis we that have unfortunately run on in the wrong way! And they were truly wise in making a better choice, which afforded them comfort in life, and now has entitled them to endless joys.

CONSIDER, *sixthly,* how much the anguish and confusion of the wicked will be increased, at the opening of the books of conscience, when the guilt of their whole lives shall be laid open to the public view of the universe. Poor sinner, what will thy thoughts be, when those crimes, which thou hast committed in the greatest secrecy, and which thou wouldst not have had known for the world; those abominations which thou imagines covered with the obscurity of night and darkness, and which thou didst flatter thyself, thy friends and acquaintance would never know; those works of iniquity, which perhaps thou couldest not find in thy heart to discover to one person, tied by all laws to a perpetual secrecy, shall all now be exposed in their true colors to the eyes of the whole world, angels and men, good and bad, to thy eternal shame. Ah Christians, it is now in your power to prevent, by a sincere repentance and confession, this confusion which you must otherwise one day suffer.

# 12

---·---

## TWELFTH DAY

### ON THE LAST SENTENCE OF THE GOOD AND BAD

CONSIDER, *first*, how this great trial shall be concluded by a final definitive sentence in favor of the just, and for the condemnation of the wicked. And first, the sovereign Judge, turning himself towards his elect, with a most sweet and amiable countenance, shall invite them into the happy mansions of everlasting bliss: *Come, ye blessed of my Father, take possession of the kingdom prepared for you from the beginning of the world.* Matt. xxv. O happy invitation! happy, thrice happy they that shall be found worthy to hear that comfortable sentence! What unspeakable satisfaction, what torrents of joy and pleasure will the hearing of it give to those blessed creatures! *I am filed with joy,* says the royal prophet, *at the happy tidings which I have heard, we are to enter into the house of the Lord,* Ps. cxxi. But, O, what envy, what rage and malice will the reprobate feel at the hearing of this invitation, when they shall see several of their acquaintance called to take possession of that eternal kingdom, which they might also have so easily purchased, had not their own folly and stupidity blindly exchanged it for the flames of hell.

CONSIDER, *secondly,* and ponder at leisure upon this happy sentence: *Come,* says the Judge, *ye blessed of my Father,* etc: Come from the vale of tears, where for a little while you have been tried and afflicted by the appointment of my providence, to the kingdom of never-ending joy; where grief and sorrow will exist no more. *Come* from the place of thy banishment, where for a time you have sighed and groaned at a distance from your heavenly country, to your everlasting home, where you shall meet with all that your heart can desire to complete your happiness; where you shall be forever inebriated with the plenty of my house, and drink forever at the fountain of life. Arise, my beloved, the winter is now past, the floods and storms are over, arise and come. O universal and eternal blessings! How my poor soul contemns all other happiness, in hopes of having a share one day in this blessed sentence!

CONSIDER, *thirdly,* how the great Judge, after having invited the just to his glorious kingdom, turning himself towards the wicked on his left hand, with fire in his eyes and terror in his countenance, shall thunder out against them the dreadful sentence of their eternal doom in these words: *Go from me you cursed into everlasting fire, which was prepared for the devil and his angels.* Christian souls, weigh well every word of this dismal sentence. *Go* forever *from me,* and from the joys of my kingdom: O terrible excommunication! O cruel divorce! O eternal banishment! Who can express, who can conceive, what it is to be forever separated from our God, our first beginning and last end, our great and sovereign good! Ah, wretches, who make so little account now of losing your God by mortal sin, what will you then think, when you shall be sentenced to this eternal banishment from him; doomed to seek him for all eternity, and yet never to meet him in any of his attributes, except his avenging justice, the weight of which you must feel forever. But take notice whither you are to go when you go from God. Alas, *into everlasting fire,* there to lead an ever-dying life, there to endure a never-ending death, in the company of the devil *and his angels;* to whom you made yourselves slaves, and who shall now without control exercise their tyranny over you forever.

CONSIDER, *fourthly,* that dreadful and universal *curse* which this just, but dismal sentence involves, *Go from me, ye cursed,* says the sovereign Judge: as if he should say, *Go, depart from me,* but take my *curse* with you. I would have given you my *blessing,* but you would not have it; a *curse* you have chosen, and a curse shall be your everlasting inheritance. It shall stick close to you, like a garment, to all eternity; it shall enter into your very bowels, and search into the very marrow of your bones. A curse upon your *eyes,* never to see the least glimpse of comfortable light: a curse on your ears, to be entertained for all eternity with the frightful shrieks and groans of the damned: a curse on your *taste,* to be forever embittered with the gall of dragons: a curse on your *smell,* to be always tormented with the noisome stench of the pit of hell: a curse on *your feeling,* and on all the members of your body, to burn and never consume in that fire which shall never be quenched: a curse upon your *understanding,* never to be illustrated with any ray of truth: a curse upon your *memory,* to be always revolving in bitterness upon a late but fruitless repentance, the shortness and vanity of past pleasures: a curse upon your *imagination,* ever representing present and future miseries: a curse upon your *will,* obstinate in evil, torn in pieces with a thousand violent, arid, withal, opposite desires, and unable to accomplish any of them: a curse, in fine, upon *your whole soul,* to be a hell to itself for all eternity! Good God, let it never be our misfortune to incur this dreadful curse!

CONSIDER, *fifthly,* how, after sentence given, the elect shall enter without delay into the possession of that everlasting kingdom, which God has prepared for those that serve him, where sorrow can have no place, and joy no end. But as for the wicked, the earth shall immediately open and swallow them all down at once, with the devils who seduced them, into the bottomless pit; and the *gate shall be shut,* never, no never, more to be opened. Behold the end of all worldly pride: behold the end of all carnal pleasure. O, how *horrid a thing it is to fall into the hands of the living God.* Heb. x.

# 13

—·—

# Thirteenth Day

## ON HELL

CONSIDER, *first,* that as it is said in holy writ, that *neither eye has been, nor ear heard, nor has it entered into the heart of man what* God *has prepared for those that serve him,* 1 Cor. ii. 9; so we may truly say with regard to hell's torments, that no mortal tongue can express them, nor heart conceive them. Beatitude, according to divines, is a *perfect and never-ending state, comprising at once all that is good, without any mixture of evil.* If then damnation be the opposite to beatitude, it must needs be a complication, an everlasting deluge of all that is evil, without the least mixture of good, the least alloy of ease, the least glimpse of comfort, a total privation of happiness, and a chaos of misery.

CONSIDER, *secondly,* in a more particular manner, what damnation is, and how many and great are the miseries it involves. *A* dying life, or rather a living death; a darksome prison, a loathsome dungeon; a binding of hand and foot in eternal chains; a land of horror and misery; a lake of fire and brimstone; a bottomless pit; devouring flames; a serpent ever gnawing; a worm never dying; a body always burning, and never consumed; a feeling always fresh for suffering; a thirst never extinguished; perpetual weeping, wailing, and gnashing of teeth. No other company but devils and damned wretches, all hating and cursing one another, all hating and cursing God; spirits always sick and in agony, yet never meeting with death which they so much desire; cast forth from the face of God into the land of oblivion, none to comfort, none to pity them; wounded to the heart with the sense of lost happiness, and oppressed with the feeling of present misery: and all these sufferings everlasting, without the least hope of end, intermission, or abatement. This is a short description, drawn for the most part from the unerring word of God, of the miseries which eternal damnation imports: this is that bitter *cup* of which *all the sinners of the earth must drink.* Psalm lxxiv.

CONSIDER, *thirdly,* that God in all his attributes is infinite: as in his power, wisdom, goodness, etc., so in his avenging justice also. He is a God as much in hell as in heaven: so that by the greatness of his love, mercy and patience here, we may measure the greatness of his future wrath and vengeance against impenitent sinners hereafter. By his infinite goodness he has drawn them out of nothing; he has preserved and sustained them for a long time; he has even come down from his throne of glory, and suffered himself to be nailed to a disgraceful cross for their eternal salvation: he has frequently delivered them from the dangers to which they were daily exposed; patiently borne with their insolence and repeated treasons; still graciously inviting them to repentance. Ah, how justly does his patience, so long abused, turn at length into fury! Mercy at last gives place to justice: and a thousand woes to those wretches, that must forever feel the dreadful weight of the avenging hand of the living God!

CONSIDER, *fourthly,* and to understand something better what hell is, set before your eyes a poor sick man lying on his bed, burning with a pestilential fever, attended with an universal pain over all his body, his head perfectly rent asunder, his eyes ready to fly out, his teeth raging, his sides pierced with dreadful stitches, his belly racked with a violent cholic, his reins with the stones and gravel; all his limbs tormented with rheumatic pains, and all his joints with the gout; his heart even bursting with anguish, and he crying out for a drop of water to cool his tongue. Can anything be conceived more miserable! and yet, let me tell you, this is but an imperfect picture of what the damned must endure for eternity: where these victims immolated to the justice of God, shall be *salted all over with fire*; and endure in all the senses and members of their body, and in all the faculties of their souls, exquisite torments!

CONSIDER, *fifthly,* that the state of the poor sick man, of whom we have just now been speaking, how deplorable soever it may seem, might still be capable of some alloy or ease, or degree of comfort: an easy bed to lie on, a goodfriend to encourage or console him, a good conscience to support him, a will resigned to the will of God, and, in fine, a certain knowledge that his pains must shortly abate, or put an end to his life. But the damned have nothing of all this. Their bed in hell is a lake or pit burning with fire and brimstone, to which they are fastened down with eternal chains: their companions are merciless devils, or what will be to them worse than devils, the unhappy partners of their sins: their conscience is ever gnawed with the worm that never dies: their will is averse from God, and continually struggling in vain with his divine will: and what comes in to complete their damnation, is a despair of ever meeting with an end or abatement of their torments. Good God, what would not a prudent man do to prevent the lying but for one night in torments in this life? And where then is our faith and reason, when we will do so little to escape the dreadful night of hell's merciless flames!

# 14

—·—

## FOURTEENTH DAY

## ON THE EXTERIOR PAINS OF HELL

CONSIDER, *first,* the description which holy Job gives us of hell, Job. x. when he calls it *a darksome land, and covered with the obscurity of death; a country of misery and darkness, where no order, but everlasting horror dwells.* In this gloomy region, no sun, moon, or stars appear; no comfortable rays of light, not even the least glimpse, are ever seen. The very fire that burneth there, contrary to the natural property of that element, is black and darksome, and affords no light to the wretches it torments, except it be to discover to them such objects as may increase their misery. Christians, what would you think, were you to be sentenced to pass the remainder of your days in some horrid dungeon, or deep hole underground, where you could never see the light! Would not death itself be preferable to such a punishment? And what is this, when compared to that eternal night to which the damned are sentenced! The Egyptians were in a sad condition, when for three days the whole kingdom was covered with dreadful darkness, caused by such gross exhalations, that they might even be felt by the hand. But this misery was soon overhand they were comforted by the return of light. Not so the damned in hell; whose night shall never have a morning, or ever expect the dawning of the day!

CONSIDER, *secondly,* that the horror of this eternal night shall be beyond measure aggravated by the dismal music wherewith those poor wretches shall be forever entertained in this melancholy abode, which shall be no other than the dreadful curses, blasphemies, and insulting voices of the tormentors, and the bowlings, groans, and shrieks of the tormented, etc. And that the other senses may also partake in their share of misery, the smell shall be forever regaled with the loathsome exhalations of those infernal dungeons, and the intolerable stench of half putrefied carcasses which are broiling there; the taste shall be oppressed with a most ravenous hunger and thirst, and the feeling with an insupportable fire.

CONSIDER, *thirdly,* that of all bodily torments, which we can suffer in this world, there is none more terrible than to burn alive: but alas, there is no comparison between burning here, and in hell. Our fires upon earth are but painted flames, if compared to the fire of hell. The fire of this world was made to serve us and be our comfort; that of hell was created to be an instrument of the vengeance of God upon sinners. The fire of this world cannot subsist without being nourished by some combustible matter, which it quickly consumes; but the fire of hell, enkindled by the breath of an angry God, requires no other fuel than sin, which feeds it without ever decaying or consuming. O, dreadful stain of sin, which suffices to maintain an everlasting fire! The fire of

this world can only reach the body: the fire of hell reaches
the soul itself and fills it with most exquisite torments. Ah,
sinners, which of you all can dwell with devouring fire?
Which of you all can endure eternal burning?

CONSIDER, *fourthly,* and to frame a just notion of hell's
torments, give ear to a most authentic vision, related by St.
Teresa, chap. xxxii. of her Life. "As I was one day," says the
Saint, "in prayer, on a sudden I found myself in hell: I know
not how I was carried thither; only I understood, that our
Lord was pleased that I should see the place which the devils
had prepared for me there, and which I had deserved by my
sins. What passed here with me lasted but a very short while;
yet if I should live many years, I do not believe I should ever
be able to forget it. The entrance appeared to me to resemble
that of an oven, very low, very narrow, and very dark.
The ground seemed like mire, exceeding filthy, stinking,
insupportable, and full of a multitude of loathsome vermin.
At the end of it there was a certain hollow place, as if it had
been a kind of a little press in a wall, into which I found
myself thrust, and close pent up. Now, though all this which
I have said was far more terrible than I have described it, yet it
might pass for a pleasure in comparison with that which I felt
in this press: this torment was so dreadful, that no words can
express the least part of it. I felt my soul burning in so dismal
a fire that I am not able to describe it. I have experienced
the most insupportable pains, in the judgment of physicians,
which can be corporally endured in this world, as well by the
shrinking up of all my sinews, as by many other torments
in several kinds: but all these were nothing in comparison

with what I suffered there: joined to the horrid thought, that this was to be without end or intermission forever: and even this itself is still little, if compared to the agony the soul is in; it seems to her that she is choaked, that she is stifled, and her anguish and torture go to a degree of excess that cannot be expressed. It is too little to say, that it seems to her that she is butchered and rent to pieces; because this would express some violence from without, which tended to her destruction; whereas here it is she herself that is her own executioner and tears herself in pieces. Now as to that interior fire and unspeakable despair which comes in to complete so many horrid torments; I know I am not able to describe them. I saw not who it was that tormented me; but I perceived myself to burn; and, at the same time, to be cut as it were and flashed in pieces. In so frightful a place, there was no room for the least hopes of comfort; there was no such thing as even sitting or lying down: I was thrust into a hole in a wall: and those horrible walls close in upon the poor prisoners, and press and stifle them. There is nothing but thick darkness without any mixture of light, and yet I know not how it is, though there be no light there, yet one sees there all that may be most mortifying to the sight.—Although it be about six years since this happened which I here relate, I am even now in writing of it so terrified, that my blood chills in my veins: so that whatsoever evils or pains I now suffer, if I do but call to my remembrance what I then endured, all that can be suffered here appears to me just nothing." So far the Saint, whose relation deserves to be pondered at leisure: for if such terrible torments had been prepared for her, whose life from her cradle (a few worldly vanities, which for a short time she had followed, excepted) had been so innocent, what must sinners one day expect?

CONSIDER, *fifthly,* that there is no man on earth, in his senses, who would be willing, even for the empire of the world, to be broiled on a gridiron like a Lawrence, or roasted for a short half hour by a slow fire, though he was sure to come off with his life; nay, where is the man that would even venture to hold his finger in the flame of a candle for half a quarter of an hour, for any reward that this world can give? Where is then the judgment of the far greater part of Christians, who pretend to believe a hell, yet live on with so little apprehension and concern, for years together, in the guilt of mortal sin; in danger every moment of falling into this dreadful and everlasting fire, having no more than a hair's breadth, that is, the thin thread of an uncertain life between their souls and a miserable eternity! Good God! deliver us from this unfortunate blindness—from this desperate fully and madness.

# 15

## FIFTEENTH DAY

## ON THE INTERIOR PAINS OF HELL

CONSIDER, *first,* that the fire of hell, with all the rest of the exterior torments, which are endured there, are terrible indeed; but no wavs comparable to the interior pains of the soul: the paena *damni,* or eternal loss of God, and of all that is good—the extremity of anguish which follows from this loss— the rueful remorse of a bitter but fruitless repentance, attended with everlasting rage and despair—the complication of all those racking tortures in the inward powers and faculties of the soul, are torments incomparably greater than anything that can be suffered in the body.

CONSIDER, *secondly,* in particular, that pain of loss, which, in the judgment of divines, is the greatest of all the torments of hell; though worldlings here have difficulties of conceiving how this can be possible. Alas! poor sinners, so weak is their notion of eternal goods, and so deeply are they immersed in the goods of this world, amusing themselves with a variety of created objects, which divert their thoughts from God's sovereign goodness, that they cannot conceive how the loss of God can be so great and dismal a torment, as his saints and servants, who are guided by better lights, agree it to be. But the case will be altered when they find themselves in hell. There they shall be convinced, by woeful experience, what misery it is to have lost their God; lost him totally; lost him irrevocably; lost him eternally; lost him in himself; lost him in all his creatures; and to be eternally banished from him, who was their only happiness, last end, sovereign good, nay, the overflowing fountain of all good: and in losing him to have lost all that is good, and that forever. As long as sinners are in this mortal life, they many ways partake of the goodness of God, *who makes the sun to rise on the good and bad, and rains upon the just and unjust.* All that is agreeable in this world, all that is delightful in creatures, and all that is comfortable in life, is all in some measure a participation of the divine goodness. No wonder then, that the sinner, whilst he so many ways partake of the goodness of God, should not in this life be sensible of what it is to be totally and eternally deprived of him. But in hell, alas! those unhappy wretches shall find, that in losing God, they have also lost all kind of good or comfort, which any of his creatures heretofore afforded; instead of which they find all things now conspiring against them, nor any way left of diverting the dreadful thought of this loss, which is always present to their minds, and gripes them with inexpressible torments.

CONSIDER, *thirdly,* that every damned soul shall be a hell to herself, and all and every one of her powers and faculties shall have their respective hells. Her memory shall be forever tormented, by revolving without ceasing on her past folly, stupidity and madness, in forfeiting the eternal joys of heaven, that ocean of bliss, which she might have obtained at so cheap a rate, and which so many of her acquaintance are now in possession of, for an empty, trifling pleasure, that lasted but for a moment, and left nothing behind but the stain of sin, and the remorse of a guilty conscience; or, for some petty interest, or punctilio of honor, by which she was then robbed of all her treasures and honors; and, upon account of which, she is now so miserably poor and despicable, eternally trodden under foot by insulting devils. Oh, what will her judgment then be of this transitory world, and all its cheating vanities, when after having been millions of ages in hell, looking back from that immense eternity, and scarce being able to find out in that infinite duration, this little point of her mortal life, she shall compare time with eternity, past pleasures with present pains, virtue with vice, and heaven with hell?

CONSIDER, *fourthly,* that the understanding of the damned shall also have its proper hell, in being forever deprived of the light of truth, always employed in false and blasphemous judgments and notions concerning God and his justice, to the great increase of its own misery; and ever dwelling upon the thoughts of present and future torments, without being able for a moment to think of anything else: so that all and every one of the torments which the damned endure, and are to endure for eternity, are every moment before the eyes of their understanding; and thus, in every moment they bear the insupportable load of a miserable eternity.

CONSIDER, *fifthly,* that as the obstinate will of the sinner
has been the guiltiest, so this power of the soul shall suffer
in proportion the greatest torment; always seeking what
she shall never find, ever flying from what she must forever
endure. Ah, what fruitless longings, what vain wishes, shall
be her constant entertainment, whilst she is doomed for
eternity, never to attain to anyone, even the least thing which
she desires! O, who can express that violent impetuosity,
with which the will of these wretches is now carried towards
God: sensible as they arc of the immense happiness which
is found in the enjoyment of him? But, alas! they always
find an invisible hand that drives them back, or rather
they always find themselves bound fast down *in* eternal
chains, struggling in vain with that hand which they cannot
resist, and unable to make the least approach towards the
object of their restless desires. Hence, they break forth
into a thousand blasphemies; hence the whole soul is torn
in pieces with a whole army of the violent, and withal
opposite passions of fury, envy, hatred, despair, etc. These
torments of the interior powers of the soul, are attended
with that never-dying worm of conscience, which shall
forever prey upon those miscreants. By which is meant an
eternal remorse, a bitter but fruitless repentance, which is
ever racking their despairing souls. Sweet Jesus, deliver us
from such a dreadful complication of evils!

# 16

## SIXTEENTH DAY

## ON A MISERABLE ETERNITY

CONSIDER, *first,* that what above all things makes hell intolerable, is the eternity of its torments, It is this eternity, which is an infinite aggravation to all and every one of them: it is this bitter ingredient which makes every drop of that bitter cup of the divine vengeance, of which the sinners of the earth must drink, so insupportable. Were there any hopes that the miseries of the damned would one day have an end, though it was after millions of ages, hell would no longer be hell, because it would admit of some comfort. But, for all those inexpressible torments to continue forever, as long as God shall be God, without the least hopes of ever seeing an end of them: oh, this it is, that is the greatest rack of the damned; O, eternity! Eternity how little do worldlings apprehend thee now! But how terrible wilt thou be to them one day, when they shall find themselves engulfed in thy bottomless abyss, there to be forever the butt and mark of all the arrows of God's avenging justice!

CONSIDER, *secondly,* if one short night seems so long and tedious to a sick man in a burning fever; if he tosses and

turns to and fro, and nowhere finds rest; if he counts every
hour, and with so much impatience longs for the succeeding
morning, whichyet will bring him but little relief or comfort
of what must this dreadful night of eternity be, accompanied
with all the interior and exterior torments of hell! No man
in his senses would purchase a kingdom at the rate of lying
for ten years on a soft bed of down, without arising from
it. Ah, what misery then must it be to be chained down to
a bed of fire and brimstone, not for ten years, nor yet for
ten thousand times ten, but for as many hundred thousand
millions of ages, as there are drops of water in the ocean,
atoms in the air; or in a word, for an immense eternity.

CONSIDER, *thirdly,* and In order to conceive still better
what this eternity is, imagine with thyself, that if any one
of the damned were to shed but one single tear at the end
of every thousand years, till he had shed tears enough to fill
the sea; what an immense space of time must this require!
The world has not yet lasted six thousand years; so that the
first of all the damned would not have shed six tears. And
yet, O dreadful eternity! the time will certainly come, when
any one of those wretches, that are now in hell, may be able
with truth to say, that, at the rate of one tear, for a thousand
years, he might have shed tears enough to drown the whole
world, and fill up the immense space between heaven and
earth: and happy would he think himself if his torments were
then to have an end. But, alas, after these millions of millions
of ages, he shall be as far from the end of his misery as he
was the first day he fell into hell. Compute after this, if thou
pleasest, as many hundred thousand millions of years as thy

thoughts can reach to; nay, suppose the whole surface of the earth to be covered with numerical figures; cast up, if thou canst, this immense sum of years, and then multiply it by itself, and multiply again a second time the product by itself, and then at the foot of this immense account write down, *Here begins eternity,* O terrible eternity! Is it possible that they who believe thee, should not fear thee? and is it possible, that they who fear thee, should dare to sin?

CONSIDER, *fourthly,* that in this eternity it would be some small comfort to the damned, if their pains, like those of this life, had any intermission or abatement. But, alas, their torments are always uniformly the same; their eternal fever never abates. For as their sins are always the same, and the gate of mercy and pardon is eternally shut against them; so the punishment of their sins shall always continue in one and the same degree of rigor, without the least remission or diminution. The rich glutton in hell, Luke xiv. has not yet been able to obtain so much as that single drop of water, for which he so earnestly begged; nor will he ever obtain it for all eternity. Nor shall length of time inure these wretches to those evils which they suffer, so as to make them the more supportable; nor shall habit or custom harden them against their acuteness; but after millions of ages their torments shall be as fresh, and their feelings of them the same as on the first day. Great God! Who can bear thy indignation or support the weight of thy avenging hand. O, dreadful evil of mortal sin, which can thus enkindle this eternal flame!

# 17

— : —

## SEVENTEENTH DAY

## ON HEAVEN

CONSIDER, *first,* that if the justice of God be so terrible in regard to his enemies, how much more will his mercy, goodness, and bounty, declare themselves in favor of his friends! Mercy and goodness are his favorite attributes, in which he most delights: *His tender mercies,* says the royal prophet, Psalm cxliv. *are above all his works.* What then must this blessed kingdom be, which in his goodness he has prepared for his beloved children, for the manifestation of his riches, glory and magnificence for all eternity. A kingdom, which the Son of God himself has purchased for us, at no less a price, than that of his own most precious blood. No wonder then that the apostle cries out, 1 Cor. ii. 9. *That neither eye hath seen, nor ear heard, nor hath it entered into the heart of man, what God has prepared for those that love him.* No wonder that this beatitude is described by divines, *as a perfect and everlasting state, replenished with all that is good, without the least mixture of evil;* a general and universal good, filling to the brim the vast capacity of our affections and desires, and eternally securing us from all fear, danger, want or change. O here it is that the servants of God, as the Psalmist declares, Psalm xxxv. *shall be inebriated with the plenty of God's house, and shall be made to drink of the torrent of his pleasure;* even of *that fountain of life,* which is with him, and flows from him, into their happy souls for ever and ever.

CONSIDER, *secondly,* that although this blessed kingdom abounds with all that can be imagined good and delightful, yet there is one sovereign good, in the sight, love, and enjoyment of which consists the essential beatitude of the soul; and that is God himself, whom the blessed shall ever see face to face; and, by the contemplation of his infinite beauty, are set on fire with seraphic flames of love, and by a most pure and amiable union are transformed in a manner into God himself: as when brass or iron in the furnace is perfectly penetrated by the fire, it loseth its own nature, and becometh all flame and fire. Happy souls! What can be wanting to complete your joys who are in perfect possession of God, the overflowing source of all good; who have within and without you, die vast ocean of endless felicity! O the excessive bounty of our God, who giveth his servants, in reward of their loyalty, so great a good, which is nothing less than himself, the immense joy of angels. O shall that not suffice, my soul, to make thee happy, which makes God himself happy!

CONSIDER, *thirdly,* the glory and beauty of the heavenly Jerusalem, which the holy scripture, to accommodate itself to our weakness, represents to us under the notion of such things as we most admire here below; so St. John in his

Apocalypse, describing this blessed city, tells us, that its walls are of precious stones, and its streets of pure and transparent gold: that these streets are watered by the river of the waters of life, resplendent as crystal, which flows from the throne of God; and that on each side the banks of this river grows the tree of life; that there shall be no night, nor any sun or moon, but that the Lord God shall be its light forever. O blessed Jerusalem! O, how *glorious* are the things *that are said of thee, O city of God!* But what wonder? For if our God has given us such, and so noble a palace here below, in this place of banishment, beautified with the sun, moon and stars, furnished and adorned with such an infinite variety of plants, flowers, trees and living creatures of so many sorts, all subservient to man; if, I say, he has so richly provided for us in this vale of tears, and region of the shade of death, what must our eternal habitation be in the land of the living! If here he is so bountiful even to his enemies, in giving them so commodious, so noble a dwelling, what may not his friends and servants expect in his eternal kingdom; in which, and by which he designs to manifest to them his greatness and glory, for endless ages, in an everlasting banquet, which he has there prepared for his elect? Blessed by all creatures be his goodness for ever.

CONSIDER, *fourthly,* the blessed inhabitants of this heavenly kingdom, those millions of millions of angels, of whom the prophet Daniel, having seen God Almighty in a vision, tells us, Dan. viii. *That thousands of thousands ministered to him, and ten thousand of hundreds of thousands stood before him:* that infinite multitude of saints and martyrs, and other servants of God of both sexes, gathered out of all nations, tribes and tongues; and above them all, the blessed Virgin Mother of God, Queen of saints and angels: their number is innumerable: but, O who can express the happiness of enjoying the society of this most noble, glorious, wise, holy and blessed company. They are all of blood royal, all kings and queens, all children and heirs of the most high God; ever beautiful and always young; crowned with wreaths of immortal glory, and shining more bright than the sun. Their love and charity for each other is more than can be conceived: they have all but one heart, will, and soul; so that the joy and satisfaction of everyone is multiplied as many fold, as there are blessed souls and angels in heaven, by the inexpressible delight each one takes in the happiness of all, and every one of the rest. O Christians, let us then imitate their virtues here, that we may enjoy their happy society hereafter, and with them eternally sing to our God the immortal songs of Sion.

CONSIDER, *fifthly,* that what renders the joys of heaven, and the felicity of its blessed inhabitants completely great, is the consideration of the duration of this bliss, and that infallible certainty and security which they enjoy; that their happiness is even linked with God's eternity; that as long as God shall be God, they shall remain with him in his blessed kingdom. O my soul, how pleasant, how delightful is it to look forward into this vast eternity, and there to lose thyself in this happy prospect of endless ages: O bless thy God, that has prepared such immortal joys for the reward of such small services, and designed them for thee from all eternity! Nor shall this immense eternity render those enjoyments the least disagreeable or tedious by the length of possession; but as God is an endless ocean of all good, and his divine essence an inexhaustible, infinite treasure of delights, so the happiness of those that eternally enjoy him shall be always fresh and always new. Conclude then, O Christian soul, to despise and forsake all that is earthly and temporal, and from this hour to begin thy journey towards this glorious, heavenly and eternal kingdom. There thou shaft find all that thy heart can desire, immortal. honors, immense riches, pure and eternal pleasures, life, health, beauty never fading, etc. O, this alone is thy true home—the land of the living.

# 18

---

# EIGHTEENTH DAY

## ON THE SMALL NUMBER OF THE ELECT

CONSIDER, *first,* those words of Christ, *Many are called but few are chosen;* which contain a great and awful truth, frequently inculcated by the mouth of truth itself, to rouse unthinking mortals from that profound lethargy, into which the enemy has lulled them. This is one of those lessons, which he has laid down for a foundation of Christian morality, in his divine sermon on the mountain, St. Matt. vii. 13, 14. where he exhorts us to, *enter in at the narrow gate, for broad is the gate, and wide is the way, that leads to damnation, and many there are that enter by it. O how narrow is the gate, and straight the way that leads to life, and few there are that find it.* Hence in the same sermon he declares that not *everyone that says to me, Lord, Lord, shall enter into the kingdom of heaven: but he that doth the will of my Father that is in heaven,* viz, by a faithful compliance with the law of God and his gospel. Without this, he assures us that it will avail us nothing, even to have done miracles in his name. *Many shall say to me on that day* (of judgment), *Lord, have we not prophesied in thy name, and cast out devils*

*in thy name, and done many wonders in thy name? And then
I will declare to them, that I never knew you, depart from
me, ye workers of iniquity.* Good God, what will become of
us, if those, that have even done miracles in thy name, shall
nevertheless be excluded thy eternal kingdom?

CONSIDER, *secondly,* how many ways this frightful truth
has been declared or prefigured in the Old Testament. Of
all the inhabitants of the earth only eight souls, viz, Noah
and his family, were preserved by the ark from the waters
of the deluge: of six hundred thousand of the children of
Israel, who came out of the land of Egypt under the conduct
of Moses, only two persons, Joshua and Caleb, entered
Canaan, the land of promise, which figure the apostle St.
Paul expressly applies to us Christians, 1 Cor. x. To the same
effect as the prophet Isaias, chap. xxiv. 13, 14. likens those
that shall escape the divine vengeance, to the small number
of olives that is left on the tree after the fruit is gathered, or
to the few branches of grapes that are found on the vines
after a well gleaned vintage. Ah Christians, hear then and
obey the voice of your Savior, who bids you, St Luke iii.
23. *Contend* (that is, strive with all your force) *to enter in
at the narrow gate, for many, I assure you, shall seek to enter
and shall not be able:* because the generality of Christians,
though they use some endeavors to enter, yet they do not
*strive* with all their force; they are not thoroughly in earnest
in their seeking, and therefore shall never find. Hear again
with fear and trembling the great apostle St. Peter, when he
tells you, that *if the just will hardly be saved, where will the
sinner appear?* First epistle, chap. iv. ver. 18. O my soul, let

us then *take care,* as the same apostle admonishes, 2 Pet. i. *By good works to make our election sure:* and if others will go in crowds to hell, let us resolve not to go with them for company sake.

CONSIDER, *thirdly,* that though the scripture had said nothing of the small number of the elect, yet that this truth must appear evident to us, if we compare the lives of the generality of Christians with the gospel of Christ, and his holy commandments. *If thou wilt enter into life,* says our Lord, Matt, xix. *keep the commandments:* there is no other way to life everlasting. And *the first and greatest of* all *the commandments,* is this, *thou shalt love the Lord thy God with all thy heart, with all thy soul, with all thy mind, and with all thy strength,* Matt. xxii. Now how few are there that keep this commandment? It is easy to *say,* with the generality of Christians, that we love God with our whole heart; but what is the *practice* of our lives? Does not self-love, vainglory, sensuality, etc, on every occasion take place? If so, it is in vain to say we *love him above all things.* And yet there is no salvation without this, love. Think well on this. Besides, the apostle James declares, chap. iv. 4. that *whosoever will be a friend of this world, becomes an enemy of God.* And St. John, epist. i. chap. ii. ver. 15. *If anyone love the world, the love of the Father is not in him.* And Christ himself declares, that we *cannot serve two masters,* Matt. vi. 24. How then can we think to reconcile the conduct of the greatest part of those who call themselves Christians (whose whole study is to please the world, and to conform themselves to its false maxims, corrupt customs, and deluded vanities) with their expectation of the kingdom of heaven, which is not to be obtained but by using violence to ourselves, by renouncing this sinful world, and by a life of self-denial and mortification?

CONSIDER, *fourthly,* how great a corruption is generally found even amongst the greatest part of true believing Christians, and from thence make a judgment of their future lot. How few are proof against human respects, and the pernicious fear of *what the world will say!* Alas, what numbers sacrifice their eternal salvation to this accursed fear, by rather choosing to forfeit the grace of God, than the false honor and esteem of this world! How many of those, whose birth and fortune have advanced them above the level of their fellow mortals, live continually in the state of damnation, by a cursed disposition of never putting up with an affront, and of preferring their worldly honor before their conscience! Unhappy men, who, by conforming themselves now to those false maxims of deluded worldlings, will be trampled underfoot by insulting devils for all eternity! How few masters of families arc sincerely solicitous for those under their charge, to see those instructions be not wanting, devotions be not neglected, etc. and that nothing scandalous or sinful lurk under the favor of their negligence or connivance! and yet the apostle assures us, that if any man neglects the care of his family, he is worse than an infidel, 1 Tim. v. 8. How few parents effectually take care to bring up their children from their infancy in the fear of God, and to inspire into them an early horror of sin above all evils! Ah, what a double damnation will the greatest part bring upon themselves, by sacrificing these tender souls to the devil and the world, which they might with so much ease has consecrated to heaven! In fine, not to run over all states of life in particular, is it not visible that injustice, impurity, pride, detraction, etc. everywhere reign among Christians; and that the number of those who live up to the gospel is very small? Good God, have mercy on us, and grant us grace to be of the number of the few, that so we may be included in the number of the saved.

# 19

— · —

## NINETEENTH DAY

### ON MORTAL SIN

CONSIDER, *first,* that there is not upon earth, nor even
in hell itself a more hideous, filthy, abominable monster,
than mortal sin: a monster, the first-born of the devil; or
to speak more properly, the parent both of the devil and
hell. There was not in the whole universe a creature more
beautiful, more perfect, more accomplished with all kinds
of gifts, both of nature and grace, than was the bright angel
Lucifer and his companions; yet one mortal sin, and that
only consented to in thought, changed them in an instant
into ugly devils, just objects of horror and abomination to
God and man. What effect then think ye will sin have upon
man, who is but dust and ashes, if it blast so foully the stars
of heaven? It was this monster, sin, that cast our first parents
out of paradise, and condemned both of them, and us their
posterity, to innumerable miseries, and to both a temporal
and eternal death. It was sin that drowned the world with
the waters of the flood! and daily crowds hell with millions
of poor souls, to be the fuel of endless flames. Good God,
deliver us from this accursed evil.

CONSIDER, *secondly,* that sin is the death of the soul. For as it is the soul of a man which gives life to his body, so consequently that body from which the soul has gone, is dead; in like manner it is the grace of God which is the life of the soul, and that soul is dead which has lost her God and his grace by mortal sin. If, then, a dead carcass, from which the soul has gone, be so loathsome and frightful, that few could endure to pass one night in the same bed with it, how is it possible, unhappy sinner, that thou canst endure to carry continually with thee the carcass of a soul dead in mortal sin, which is far more loathsome and hideous! Ah, beg of God that he would open thy eyes to see thine own deplorable state, to detest the hellish monster sin, which thou hast so long nourished in thy breast, and which is the true cause of all thy misery.

CONSIDER, *thirdly,* what the soul loses by sin, and what she gains in recompence of this loss. She loses the grace of God, the greatest of all treasures; and in losing this, she loses God himself. She loses the fatherly protection and favor of God; she loses the dignity of a child of God, and spouse of Christ; she forfeits her right and title to an eternal kingdom; she is strip of all the gifts of the Holy Ghost, robbed of all the merits of her whole life; becomes a child of hell, and a slave of the devil; spiritually possessed by him, and with him liable to eternal damnation: this is all she gains by sin: because *the wages of sin is death, Rom.* vi. the death of the soul here, and a second and eternal death hereafter; Ah, wretched sinners, open your eyes to see, and bewail your lamentable blindness, in thus exchanging God for the devil, heaven for hell.

CONSIDER, *fourthly,* that sin is infinitely odious and detestable in the sight of God, as being infinitely opposite to his sovereign goodness. He hates it with an eternal and necessary hatred; and can no more cease to bate it, than he can cease to be just. Hence if the most just man upon earth were so unhappy, as to fall into the least mortal sin, he would in that instant become the enemy of God, and were he to die in the guilt thereof, he would certainly feel the weight of God's avenging justice for all eternity. Ah, Christians, never let us be so mad as to venture to wage war with God. Alas, how many dreadful judgments does he daily exercise upon sin and sinners? How many, in punishment of sin, arc snatched away in the flower of their age, by sudden and unprovided death? How many die in despair? How many, after having long abused God's graces, are given up to a reprobate sense, to hardness of heart, the worst and most terrible of all his judgments? O, let us tremble at the thoughts of so great a misfortune; let us be convinced, that there can be no misery so great as that which we incur by mortal sin; and that we are more our own enemies, and do ourselves more mischief, by consenting to any one mortal sin, than all the men upon earth, and all the devils in hell could do us, though they were all to conspire together to do their worst: because all they can do, so long as we refuse consent to sin, cannot hurt the soul, whereas by consenting to one mortal sin, we bring upon our own souls a dreadful and eternal death. Good God, never suffer us to be so blinded as to become thus the murderers of our own souls.

CONSIDER, *fifthly*, O my soul, and tremble at the
multitude of thy treasons against God, by which thou hast
so often provoked his indignation during the whole course
of thy life. Alas, is it not too true, that no sooner didst thou
come to the use of reason, than thou didst abandon thy king
and thy God, under the wings of whose fatherly protection
thou hadst happily passed the days of thy innocence? Ah,
how early didst thou run away from the best of fathers,
and like the prodigal son squandering away thy substance
in a strange land, hast sought in vain to satisfy thy appetite
with the husks of swine. Recall to thy remembrance, in
the bitterness of thy soul, all the years of thy past life; and
see what treasures of iniquity, in thought, word, and deed,
will discover themselves to thy eyes: see how long thou hast
unconcernedly sported on the brink of a dreadful precipice,
having no more than a hairs breadth betwixt thy soul and
hell. Be confounded at thy past folly; admire and adore the
goodness of thy God; and now at least resolve to embrace his
mercy.

# 20

---

## TWENTIETH DAY

### ON THE RELAPSING SINNER

CONSIDER, *first,* that if one mortal sin be so heinous a treason against the sovereign majesty of God, as we have seen in the foregoing chapter; if every such sin be an abomination to our Lord, and the death of that unhappy sinner whose guilty of it, what must we think of the miserable condition of *relapsing sinners,* that is, of such Christians as are continually falling again and again into the same mortal sins, after repeated confessions and solemn promises of amendment? Alas, what can we think, but that by this method of life they are treasuring up to themselves wrath against the day of wrath: and will in all appearance, sooner or later, draw down a dreadful vengeance upon their own heads. Because by every relapse their crime is aggravated, and their latter condition becomes worse than the former.

CONSIDER, *secondly,* the ingratitude, the perfidiousness, the contempt of God, which the relapsing sinner is guilty of, as often as, after his reconciliation, he returns like a dog to the vomit. He is guilty of the highest ingratitude, in treading underfoot the grace of reconciliation, by which he had been a little before raised from the dunghill of sin, and even drawn out of the jaws of hell; and by a distinguishing mercy restored to the friendship of God, to the dignity of a child of God, and heir of heaven. He is guilty of a base perfidiousness, in breaking his solemn word given to God in his confession. He is guilty of a notorious contempt of the Divine Majesty, in banishing God from his soul, after having invited him in, and introducing Satan in his place; and this after a full knowledge and experience of both sides. Good God, to putthe whole universe in balance with thee, would be a most heinous affront; since heaven, and all the powers thereof, the earth and seas, and all things therein, are less than a grain of sand, if compared to thee: what then must we think of the unparalleled injury done thee by the relapsing sinner, when putting thee and Satan in the scales, ne gives the preference to the Devil.

CONSIDER, *thirdly,* the dreadful danger to which the relapsing sinner is daily exposed, from the sword of the Divine Justice hanging over his guilty head, and daily provoked by his ingratitude and insolence. Alas, we are all mortal; we neither know the day nor the hour that will be our last; if we be surprised by death in the state of mortal sin, as millions have been, we arc irrecoverably lost. If then it be madness at any time to risk eternity by consenting to mortal sin, how much more to provoke the Almighty by frequent relapses, and by a practice of abusing his grace and mercy at every turn? Ah, what multitudes of souls have been thus betrayed into that dismal pit of never-ending wo, where the worm never dies, and the fire never is quenched! Unhappy wretches! they designed as little to damn themselves, as any of us; but God will not be laughed at.

CONSIDER, *fourthly,* another evil which the sinner, who frequently falls back into the same sins, has too just reason to apprehend, is the insincerity of his past repentance. For, in reality, what appearance is there that his sorrow and resolution of amendment have been such as God requires, when after so many confessions he is still the same man? True contrition is a sovereign grief, by which the penitent detests bis sin above all other evils, with a full determination and find resolution of never returning to it anymore. Now how is it likely, that the relapsing sinner detests sincerely his sin above all evils, with a firm purpose of amendment, when he is so easily prevailed upon by the first temptation to return to it again.

CONSIDER, *fifthly*, the remedies and means by which we are to be preserved from this pernicious evil of relapsing into mortal sin. The first is to avoid the dangerous occasions, which have or probably may draw us into the same sins: without this care to fly the occasions of sin, the strongest resolution of amendment will prove ineffectual, as we daily see by woeful experience: for *he that loves the danger shall perish in it,* Eccl. iii. No pretexts of worldly concerns must here be put in the balance with eternity: we must part with hand or eye, sooner than lose our souls. Another main preservative against relapse, is to labor by fervent prayer, and diligent frequenting of the sacraments, to suppress the unhappy dispositions that insensibly lead thereunto; vigorously to resist the first motions to evil; and to strive with all possible diligence to root out that wretched propensity to sin, which former sins have left in the soul. Ah, how hard it is to maintain a castle, where the enemy has already surprised the avenues, and has a strong party within, ready to open the gates to him! The third and chief remedy against relapse, is for the penitent to nourish carefully in his heart a truly penitential spirit, daily to renew his sorrow for his sins, and to recount in the sight of God, in the bitterness of his soul, all his past iniquities; daily to admire and adore that mercy, which has borne with him so long, and to value above all treasures that grace of reconciliation, by which he has been drawn out of so much misery; daily to beg of God with all the fervor of his soul, sooner to take him out of this world, than to suffer him any more to die by mortal sin. Good God, grant that this may be always the disposition of our souls. *Amen. Amen.*

# 21

—·—

## TWENTY-FIRST DAY

## ON DOING PENANCE FOR OUR SINS

CONSIDER, *first,* those words of Christ, Luke xiii. 3, 5. *Except you do penance, you shall all perish.* Behold here a general rule, nor does our Lord make any exception. Penance then is necessary, *first,* for all those whose conscience accuses them of mortal sin: alas, such as these must either do penance for their sins or burn for them for all eternity! Poor sinners! Their state is most deplorable! they are playing upon the brink of hell, and every moment one or other of them is tumbling into that bottomless pit; and is it possible they should be unconcerned under so great and evident a danger? Why then do they not lay hold of the grace of penance, the only plank that can save them after shipwreck; the only means left for the salvation of their souls. *Secondly,* Penance is necessary for all those, who, though their conscience accuses them not at present, yet have in their past life been guilty of such mortal offences. Ah, Christians, one mortal sin is enough for us to do penance, for all our life. And how can we do less, if we consider what mortal sin is; what it is to have been the enemies of God; what it is to have been under the sentence of eternal damnation; and never certainly to know whether this sentence has been cancelled? Is not this sufficient to oblige us to a penitential life? Can we otherwise pretend to be secure? Even these (and God best knows how few they are) who are not conscious to themselves of having committed such a sin in their whole lifetime, must not therefore think themselves exempt from the obligation of doing penance; as well because of their hidden sins, as of those which they may have occasioned in others; for *no man knows whether he be worthy of love or hatred,* Eccl. viii. 9. as also, because a penitential life is the best security against sin, which will insensibly prevail over us, if not curbed by self-denial, mortification, and penance.

CONSIDER, *secondly,* that as in the method of penance, different rules must be prescribed to different persons. Those who have the misfortune to be actually in the state of mortal sin, or what is still more deplorable, are plunged in the depth of a habit of one or more kinds of mortal sins, as soon as their eyes are opened to discover the hellish monster which they carry about with them, must, like the prodigal child, arise without delay, to return to their Father. A sacrifice of a contrite and humble heart is what God above all things requires at their hands; this ought to be the foundation of all their penance: without this, corporal austerities will be of small account. Such sinners ought to give themselves no rest, till they have made their peace with God: their sins ought to be always before their eyes. Their first thoughts in the morning ought to be upon their misfortune, in being at so great a distance from God, enslaved to the devil, and liable to be his companions in eternal misery: the like ought to be their last thoughts at night; when, like the penitent David, they ought to wash their beds with their tears. As often as they appear before their God in prayer, it ought to be in the spirit of the humble publican, looking upon themselves as unworthy to lift up their eyes to heaven, or towards the altar of God; and with him, striking their breasts, with a *Lord be merciful to me a sinner.* Thus, will they certainly obtain mercy from him, who is the father of mercy.

CONSIDER, *thirdly,* that after the sinner has done his best endeavors to seek a reconciliation with his offended God, by a sincere repentance and confession of his sins, he must not think himself exempt from any further penance, as if he had now no just debt to discharge to the justice of God, no obligation of making satisfaction for his sins by penitential works, and of bringing forth fruits worthy of penance. This would be a great and dangerous error. Nor must he content himself with barely quitting himself of the penance enjoined by his confessor, which is to be feared seldom is sufficient to satisfy the justice of God. Alas, if sinners were truly sensible of the enormous injury done to God by mortal sin, as true penitents must be, they would certainly do penance in another manner, than too many do; they would be more in earnest in chastising their sinful flesh by penitential works, and thus making a more proportionable satisfaction for their past treasons.

CONSIDER, *fourthly,* that the time manner of doing penance for our sins, is better learnt from the holy fathers and doctrines of the church, than from the loose maxims of worldlings, or the practice of too many penitents in this degenerate age. Let us give ear then to those lights of the church and follow their directions on this important subject. "God himself has taught us," says St. Cyprian, (L. de Lapsis) "in what manner we are to crave mercy of him. He himself says, *Return to me with your whole heart, in fasting, and weeping, and mourning,* Joel ii. "Let us then return to the Lord with our whole heart; let us appease his wrath by fasting, weeping and mourning, as he admonishes us. Let the greatness of our grief equal the heinousness of our sins.—We must pray earnestly, we must pass the day in mourning, and the night in watching and weeping, spending all our time in penitential tears. Our lodging should be on the floor strewed with ashes; our covering hair cloth, etc. After having cast off the garment of Christ, we should not now seek any (worldly) clothing.—We must employ ourselves now in good works, by which our sins may be purged away. We must give frequent alms, by which our souls may be delivered from death." So far St. Cyprian. With whom agrees St. Pacian, in his exhortation to penance: "If any one call you to the bagnio, you must renounce all such delights. If anyone invite you to a banquet, you must say, such invitations are for those that have not had the misfortune to lose their God. I have sinned against the Lord and am in danger of perishing eternally. What have I to do with feasts, that have offended my God? You must make your court to the poor; you must beg the prayers of widows; you must cast yourself at the feet of the priests; you must implore the intercession of the church: you must try all means, which may prevent your perishing everlastingly." And St. Ambrose, in his second book of penance, chap. x. "Can anyone imagine that he is doing penance, whilst he is indulging his ambition in the pursuit of honors, whilst he is following wine, etc. The true penitent must renounce the world, must abridge even the necessary time of sleep, must interrupt it with his sighs, and cut it short with his prayers." And St. Caesarins of Arles, Hom. viii. "As often as we visit the sick, or those that are in prison, or reconcile together those that are at variance with one another; as often as we fast on days commanded by the church—give alms to the poor that pass by our door, etc. By these, and such like works, our small sins are redeemed daily. But this alone is not enough for capital crimes; we must add tears and lamentations, and long fasts; and give large alms to the utmost of our power." Thus, as the same saint tells us, Hom. i. "By present mortification will be prevented the future sentence of eternal death: thus by humbling the guilty will the guilt be consumed: and by this voluntary severity, the wrath of a dreadful Judge will be appeased—These short, penitential labors will pay off those vast debts, which otherwise everlasting burning will never be able to discharge." Christians, let us follow in practice these excellent guides.

# 22

## Twenty-second Day
### AGAINST DELAY OF REPENTANCE

CONSIDER, *first,* that of all the deceits by which Satan deludes sinners to their eternal ruin, there is none greater or more dangerous than when he persuades them to put off their repentance and conversion from time to time, till no more time remains for repentance. Alas! thousands and millions of poor souls have been thus betrayed into everlasting flames, who never designed to damn themselves by dying in sin, any more than we do at present. But, by putting off their conversion, they have, by a just judgment of God, been surprised by death, when they least expected it; and, dying as they lived, have been justly sentenced to that second and everlasting death. Unhappy wretches! who would not believe their just Judge, who so often cautions them to watch; and declares in the gospel, that otherwise he shall come at a time when they least expect him. Ah, how dreadful and how common are these unprovided deaths!

CONSIDER, *secondly,* the great presumption of sinners, who put off their reconciliation with an offended God till another time, shutting their ears to his voice, by which he calls them at present, and refusing him entrance into their hearts, where he stands and knocks. Alas, if he withdraws himself, they are undone for ever: how dare they then treat him with so much contempt? Is it not an infinite goodness, and inexpressible condescension in this sovereign Majesty, to call after them, when they are running from him; and so earnestly to press them, without any interest on his side, to return to him who is their only good, and supreme happiness? What then ought they not to apprehend from his justice, if they obstinately and insolently refuse to embrace his mercy? How dare they pretend to dispose of the time to come, or promise themselves greater graces hereafter, than those which they now abuse? Do they not know that God alone is master of time and grace, and that by his just judgment those who presume to tempt him in this manner, generally speaking, die in their sins? Ah, it is too true, that he who has promised pardon to the sinner that is sincerely converted, has neither promised time nor efficacious grace to those who defer their conversion.

CONSIDER, *thirdly,* the great folly of sinners, who put off their conversion to God till another time, upon pretense of doing it more easily hereafter: whereas, both reason and experience make it evident, that the longer they defer this work, the more difficulties they meet to compass it. And how can it be otherwise, since by this delay, and by adding daily sin to sin, their sinful habits gather strength; the devil's power over them increases; and God, who is daily more and more provoked, is by degrees less liberal of his graces, so that they become less frequent and pressing: till at length, by accustoming themselves to resist his grace, they fall into the wretched state of blindness and hardness of heart, the broad road to final impenitence!

CONSIDER, *fourthly,* the unparalleled madness of those who defer their conversion upon the confidence of a death-bed repentance; designing to put a cheat upon the justice of God, by indulging themselves in sin all their lifetime; and then making their peace with God, when they can sin no longer. Unhappy wretches! consider that God *is not to be mocked: that what a man soweth, the same shall he reap,* Gal. vi. 6. The general rule is, that as a man lives, so he dies: a rule so general, that in the whole scripture we have but *one example* of a person who died well after a wicked life, viz. *the good thief;* an example so singular in all its circumstances, as to give no encouragement to sinners who entertain a premeditated design of cheating the justice of God by a death-bed conversion. Ah, how dreadfully difficult must it be for a dying sinner, in whom the habit of sin is by long custom turned into a second nature, to attain to a thorough change of heart, sincere sorrow and detestation of sin, love of God above all things, which he never thought of in his life-time; and which now become indispensably necessary. Ah, how deceitful are those tears, which arc often shed by dying sinners, (as may be seen in the case of King Antiochus,) which being wholly influenced by the fear of deaths prevail not with the just Judge. And if there be so much danger, even when tears are plentifully shed, what must there be, when, as it commonly happens, either the dullness and stupidity caused by the sickness, or the pains and agonies of the body and mind, are so great, as to hinder any serious application of the thoughts to the greatest of all concerns? For if a headache be enough to hinder us from being able to pray with any devotion, what an obstacle to prayer must not the agonies of death be? No wonder then, that the saints and servants of God make so little account of those death-bed performances. Especially since, as we see by daily experience, that those who made the greatest shew of repentance, when they were in danger of death, no sooner escaped that danger, but are still the same men they were before. O Christians, let us not then be imposed upon by the false and flattering discourses of men, who are so free in pronouncing favorably of all those, who after a life spent in sin, make some shew of repentance at their death. Let us rather tremble at the deplorable case of such souls; and remember that the judgments of God are very different from those of men.

# 23

—·—

## TWENTY-THIRD DAY

## ON TIME AND ETERNITY

CONSIDER, *first,* how precious a thing time is, which we are apt to squander away, as if it were of no value. Time is the measure of our lives, and as much as we lose of our time, so much of our life is absolutely lost. Time is given us to gain eternity; and there is not one moment of time, in which we may not work for eternity; and in which we may not store up immense and everlasting treasures. As many therefore as we lose of these precious moments, are so many lost eternities. The present is the only time of working: it is the only time we can call our own, and God only knows how long it will last. It is short, it flies away in an instant, and when once it is gone, it cannot be recalled; the very moment in which we are reading this line, is just passing, never, no, never more to return. Every hour is posting away, without stopping one moment till it be swallowed up in the immense gulf of eternity: and as many of these hours or moments as are lost, are Jost for ever; the loss is irreparable. Learn hence, O my soul, to set a just value upon the present time; learn to husband it well, by employing it in good works.

CONSIDER, *secondly,* Christian soul, what thy thoughts
will be, at the approach of death, of the value of time, which
thou makest so little account of at present. What wouldest
thou not then give for some of those hours which now thou
losest in vanity and sin? Ah, the dreadful anguish that will
rack the soul of the dying sinner, when seeing himself at the
brink of a miserable eternity, he shall wish a thousand times,
but in vain, that he could recall one day, or even one hour of
his past time, and bad but the same health and strength as he
formerly had, to employ it in the love of God, and sincere
repentance for his sins. Ah, worldlings, why are yon then
so blind as not to see, that any one of these hours, which
you daily squander away, is indeed, more valuable than ten
thousand worlds.

CONSIDER, *thirdly,* what will be the sentiments of the
damned of the value of time, when time shall be no more:
how bitterly will they regret during eternity, all those hours,
days, months and years, which were allowed them by the
bounty of their Creator, during the space of their mortal life;
by the due employment of which, they might have prevented
that misery, to which they are now irrevocably condemned;
and might have made themselves eternally and infinitely
happy; but, alas, they would not work whilst the time was,
whilst they had the day-light before them: the night, the
dismal and eternal night is now come, in which it is too late
to work; and during which, they shall eternally condemn
their past folly and madness, in neglecting and abusing their
precious time. Ah, Christians, let us be wise at their expense.
But what do you think will be the sentiments of the blessed

in heaven of this precious time? Truly, if it were possible, and if their happy state could admit of such a thing as grief, there is nothing those blessed souls would regret more than the loss of any of those moments, which in their life-time had hot been well husbanded: when they shall clearly see, in the light of God, what an immense increase of glory and happiness they might have acquired, by the due employment of those precious moments.

CONSIDER, *fourthly,* that as all time is short, and passes quickly away, so all temporal enjoyments, honors, riches, and pleasures of this world, are all transitory, uncertain, and inconstant. Only eternity, and the goods or evils which it comprises, are truly great, as being without end, without change, without comparison, admitting of no mixture of evil in its goods, nor any alloy of comfort in its evils. O the vanity of all temporal grandeur, which must so soon be buried in the coffin. O how quickly does the glory of this world pass away? A few short years are more than anyone can promise himself: and after that, poor sinner, what will become of thee? Alas, the worms will prey upon thy body, and merciless devils on thy unrepenting soul. Thy worldly friends will forget thee; the very stones, on which thou hast got thy name engraved, will not long out-live thee. O how true is that sentence, *Vanity of vanities, and all is vanity: but to love God, and to serve him alone*? [a Kempis.] It is thus only we shall be wise for eternity; all other wisdom is but folly.

# 24

---

## Twenty-Fourth Day

### ON THE PRESENCE OF GOD

CONSIDER, first, that God is everywhere present. *If I ascend into heaven,* says the Psalmist, Psalm cxxx. 8. *thou art there; if I descend into hell, thou art there,* He fills both heaven and earth: and there is no created thing whatsoever, in which he is not truly and perfectly present. In him we live, in him we move; our very being is in him. As the birds, wherever they fly, meet with the air, which encompasses them on all sides, and the fishes swimming in the ocean everywhere meet with the waters: so we, wherever we are, or wherever we go, meet with God; we have him always with us; he is more intimately present to our souls, than our souls are to our bodies. Alas, poor soul of mine, how little have we thought of this? And yet it is an article of our faith, in which we have been instructed from the very cradle. Let us seriously reflect on this truth for the future: let us strive to be always with him, who is always with us.

CONSIDER, *secondly,* that God being everywhere, sees us wherever we are; all our actions are done in his sight; our very thoughts, even the most secret motions and dispositions of our hearts, cannot be concealed from his all-seeing eye. In vain does the sinner flatter himself in his crimes like the libertine mentioned by the wise man, Eccl. xxiii. that *darkness encompasses him, and walls cover him, and no one sees him whom he fears.* Alas, *the eyes of the Lord are infinitely brighter than the rays of the sun;* and no darkness, clouds, walls or curtains, can screen us from his piercing sight, which penetrating clearly sees the very center of the soul; and no wonder that he should clearly see what passes in the place where he is always present.

CONSIDER, *thirdly,* that God, who is in all places, and in all things, is everywhere whole and entire, because he is indivisible; he is everywhere with all his majesty, attributes and perfections. We have then within us, O my soul, the eternal, immense, omnipotent, self-existent, infinite Lord and Maker of all things; and we are within this infinite Being, who accompanies us wherever we go. He is in all places with his omnipotence, to which all things are subject; what then have his friends to fear? He is everywhere with his infinite justice; how then can his enemies be secure? He is everywhere infinitely good to his children; his love and kindness to them surpasses that of the most tender mother; his providence watches over them, his wisdom wonderfully disposes of all things for their greater good: O what comfort then, must this thought of the presence of God afford his servants, and those that truly fear and love him?

CONSIDER, *fourthly,* that God existing in all places, requires of us that we should everywhere take notice of his presence. Can there be any object more worthy of our attention? And shall we then be so unfortunately blind as to amuse ourselves with every trifle that falls in our way, and let God, the sovereign beauty, and sovereign good, pass unregarded? Ah, let us never regret being alone, since we have always in our company that infinite Being, the sight and enjoyment of whom is the eternal felicity of angels. What if we see him not with our corporal eyes, is he the less present? But have we not more noble eyes, viz. the eyes of the understanding, which, assisted by divine faith, ought to contemplate God, always present in the very midst of us? Ah, the sweetest repose is to be found in him; all other recreations are vain, when compared to this.

CONSIDER, *fifthly,* that God being everywhere present, it is requisite that we should comport ourselves, interiorly and exteriorly, in such manner as becomes those who are standing, in his sight. The presence of a person, for whom we have a respect, is sufficient to restrain us from doing anything trivial or indecent: and shall not the presence of the infinite majesty of God, in comparison with whom the greatest monarchs of the earth are less than nothing, restrain us in that exterior modesty and interior reverence which is so justly its due? Ought we not even to annihilate ourselves in the sight of this immense Divinity? But, O my God, how far are we from these dispositions, as often as we dare to sin in thy almighty presence, and fly in the face of thy sovereign Majesty! Alas, my poor soul, how should we be ashamed to have our sins known to such persons, whose esteem we covet? We should be ready even to die with confusion to have them known to the whole world. We should be very unwilling to have even our vain and ridiculous amusements, though otherwise innocent, laid open to the eyes of our neighbors. And why will we consider the all-seeing eye of our great God, which is always fixed upon us, and clearly discerns all that passes in the most secret closet of our heart? Why will we not reflect that our evil thoughts being known to God, is indeed a greater shame, a greater loss of our true honor, than if they were published by sound of trumpet over the universe.

CONSIDER, *sixthly,* that God, being everywhere present, everywhere requires our love: he is everywhere infinitely amiable, beautiful, good, perfect, and at all times and in every place he is infinitely good to us. Why then do we not love him who is all love? *Deus charitas est,* says St. John, 1 John iv. *God is love.* We have this loving and most lovely God continually with us and within us; why do we not inn to his embraces? He is a fire that ever burns in the very center of our souls; how then comes it to pass that we feel so little of its flames? It is because we do not approach it. It is because we will not restrain our thoughts at home, attentive to that great guest who resides within us, but sutler them continually to wander abroad upon vain created amusements. O, *convertere, anima mea, in requiem tuam,* Ps. cxliv. Turn away, my soul, from all these worldly to vs, which keep thee at a distance from thy God; return then to him who is thy true and only happiness, for in him only thou wilt find everlasting repose.

# 25

— · —

## TWENTY-FIFTH DAY

### ON THE PASSION OF CHRIST AND FIRST: ON OUR SAVIOR IN THE GARDEN OF GETHSEMANE

CONSIDER, *first,* how the Son of God, (who came down from heaven, and clothed himself with our humanity, in order to be our priest and our victim, and to offer himself a bleeding sacrifice for our sins to his eternal Father,) was pleased to begin his passion by a bloody sweat and agony in the garden of Gethsemani, the night before his death. Here having left the rest of his disciples at Some distance, and taking with him Peter, James and John, who before had been witnesses of his glorious transfiguration on mount Thabor, he begins to disclose to them that mortal anguish, fear and sadness, which oppressed his heart. *My soul,* saith he, *is sad even unto death,* Matt. xxvi. That is, with a sadness, which even now would strike me dead, if I did not preserve myself, in order to suffer still more for you. Sweet Jesus, what can be the meaning of this? Didst thou not lately cry out, speaking of thy passion, and the desire that thou hadst of suffering for us: *I have a baptism wherewith I am to be baptized, and how am I straitened till it be accomplished,* Luke xii. Whence then comes this present *sadness*? Was it not thou, who hast given that strength or courage to thy martyrs, as not even to shrink under the worst of torments? And art thou thyself *afraid?* But, O dear Lord, 1 plainly understand that it was by thy own choice, that thou hast condescended so far, as to let thyself be seized by this mortal anguish. It was for my instruction; and that thou mightest suffer so much the more for my sake, I adore thee under this weakness (if 1 may be allowed to call it so) no less than on thy throne of glory; because it is here, that I better discover thy infinite love for me,

CONSIDER, *secondly,* how our dear Savior under this anguish and sadness betakes himself to prayer, as the only refuge under afflictions, the only shield in the day of battle. But take notice, my soul, with what reverence he prays, prostrate on the very ground, to nis eternal Father; and with what fervor; *with a loud cry and tears,* says the Apostle, Heb. v. 7. Learn then to imitate him. In this prayer he condescended so far as to allow the inferior part to petition, that the cup of his bitter passion might be removed from him: but then he immediately added; *yet not my will, but thine be done.* To teach us, under all trials and crosses, a perfect submission, and resignation to the divine will.

CONSIDER, *thirdly,* how our Savior interrupted twice his prayer to come and visit his disciples but found them both times asleep. Ah, my soul, and is it not thy case also to sleep, that is, to indulge thyself in a slothful, sensual way of living; whereas the whole life of thy Savior was spent in laboring for thy salvation; and that all he then suffered, he suffered for thee. Ah, pity now at least his comfortless condition, whilst on the one hand his Father seems deaf to his prayers, and on the other his disciples are too drowsy to afford him the least attention. In this desolate state an angel from heaven appears to comfort Him, who is the joy of angels. O what humility! But what kind of comfort, think you, did this angel bring? No other but the representing to him the will of his eternal Father, and humbly entreating him, in the name of heaven and earth, not to decline the imparting to poor sinners, by his infinite love, the plentiful redemption, for which he came into the world, and to undergo the ignominies and torments of one short day's continuance, in a prospect of the salvation of mankind, and of that eternal glory and honor which the Godhead should receive from his sufferings. Let the like consideration of the will of God, his greater honor and glory, and the good of thy own soul, comfort thee also under all thy anguish and crosses. There can be no comfort more solid.

CONSIDER, *fourthly,* the mortal agony which our Savior suffered in his soul this night during his prayer. We may judge of its pains and anguish by the wonderful effect they produced in his body, by casting him into so prodigious a sweat of blood, as to imbrue the very ground on which he lay prostrate. Sweet Jesus, who ever heard of such an agony? But what thinkest thou, my soul, was the true cause of all this anguish, and bitter agony of thy Savior? Chiefly these: *first,* A clear view and lively representation of all that he was to suffer during the whole course of his passion: so that all the ignominies and torments, that he was afterwards successively to undergo, were now all at once presented before the eyes of his soul, with all their respective aggravations; by which means he suffered his whole bitter passion twice over, once by the hands of his enemies, and another time by his own most clear and lively imagination of all that he had to suffer. But why, dear Jesus, these additional agonies? 'Tis only thy love can answer. Another cause that contributed to our Savior's anguish, was a distinct view of the sins of the whole world from the first to the last; of the horrid crimes and abominations of mankind, all now laid to his charge, to be cancelled by the last drop of his blood. Ah, how hideous, how detestable were all these hellish monsters, in the eyes of our Savior, who alone had a just notion of their enormity, by having always before him a clear sight of the infinite majesty by them offended! O Lord, how great a share has not my sins had in this tragical scene 1 how much, alas, did they contribute to thy pains and grief? A third cause of our Savior's agony, was the foreknowledge he had of the little use Christians would make of all his sufferings. He foresaw that blindness and hardness of heart, by which they would pervert this antidote into a mortal poison and tread his precious blood under their feet; as well as the eternal loss of so many millions of souls, for which he was to die. All these sad and melancholy thoughts assailing at once the soul of our Redeemer, cast him into a mortal agony, and forced from him those streams of blood. Ah, Christians, pity now the anguish of your Savior and resolve never more to have any hand in afflicting his tender soul by sin.

# 26

———•———

# TWENTY-SIXTH DAY

## ON OUR SAVIOUR IN THE COURT OF CAIPHAS

CONSIDER, *first,* how our Savior arising from his prayer, after having conquered all his fears, returns to his disciples, bidding them now sleep on and take their rest, for that his hour was come, and that the traitor was just at hand. But thou, dear Lord, when wilt thou enjoy rest or sleep? Not till the last sleep of death on the hard bed of the cross. Contemplate, Christians, the courage and readiness which our Savior shews to suffer for you, by going forth to meet the traitor and his band. Behold with what meekness he receives the treacherous kiss of peace. And yet, to make it evident that no power upon earth could arrest him but with his own free will, with the force of two words, *Ego sunt, I am he,* he struck down the whole multitude that was come to apprehend him, making them all reel backward, and fall to the ground. After which he delivered himself into their hands; and they having bound him, dragged him along into the city, whilst his disciples fled and abandoned him, leaving him in the hands of his enemies, who presented him first before Annas, the father-in-law of the high-priest, where he was insulted by a vile servant, who struck him on the face. From thence they led him to the court of Caiphas, where the chief priests and elders were assembled, longing to see this new prisoner before them, determined to make away with him, right or wrong. Follow thou thy Savior, O my soul, now abandoned by all his friends: contemplate this meek lamb, loaded with their scoffs and insults, in the midst of ravenous wolves: but carry the eyes of thy understanding still farther: view the interior of his soul, and see the joy and satisfaction he takes in complying with the will of his eternal Father, and suffering for thee: and learn from hence to have the like dispositions in all thy sufferings.

CONSIDER, *secondly,* how our Lord was no sooner brought to the court of Caiphas the high-priest, where the great council of the Sanhedrim was assembled, but immediately after a scornful welcome they proceed to his trial, and call in the false witnesses, who were to depose against him. But behold the providence of God, see the force of truth, and the wonderful innocence of this Lamb of God; notwithstanding the malice of this impious court and their witnesses, men of neither honor nor conscience, yet all that they could allege against him was either insignificant, or they could not agree in their story, which made their testimonies of no weight. But whilst thou adores this providence, behold and admire the meekness and patience of thy Savior, who remained silent under all the provocations given by these false witnesses; giving thereby a most convincing proof of his being more than man, who could thus calmly hold his peace, whilst his reputation and life were both attacked by palpable

calumnies. The malice of our Savior's enemies being thus
confounded, the high-priest arises, and adjures him by the
living God, to tell him if he was the Christ, the Son of
God! In reverence to which adorable name, our Lord made
a solemn confession and profession of the truth, teaching by
his example, all his followers, when called to the like trial,
never to be ashamed of him, or his faith. Upon this, Caiphas
rends his garments, crying out, *Blasphemy!* And they all
pronounce him w*orthy of death.* But thou, my soul, let us,
on the contrary, cry out with the angels, and all the elect of
God, Rev. v. 12. *The Lamb that was slain, is worthy to receive
power, and divinity, and wisdom, and strength, and honor,
and glory, and benediction,* from all creatures forever.

CONSIDER, *thirdly,* how that unjust sentence against our
Redeemer was np sooner pronounced by the great council,
but immediately they all, with unheard of barbarity, fell
upon him, more like furies of hell than men, discharging
upon him all kinds of injuries, blows, affronts and
blasphemy. See, my soul, how these hell-hounds spit in the
face of thy Savior, and disgorge their filthy phlegm on that
sacred forehead where beauty and majesty sits: behold how
they bullet, kick, and strike him with merciless rage, whilst
he, with his hands tied behind him, is not able to ward
off one blow, nor has any friend present to wipe his face,
or afford him any other help. See, how they muffle up his
face with a filthy rag, and then in derision (as if he were a
mock-prophet or impostor) at every blow bid him prophesy
who it was that struck him: besides many other affronts,
which he endured with an invincible patience and fortitude.

CONSIDER, *fourthly,* that of all our Savior's sufferings in the court of Caiphas, none touched him so much to the quick as the fall of Peter, the chief of his apostles, who had received the most signal favors from him. Who, after having boasted that very night, that though all the rest of the disciples should abandon their Master, he would never forsake him; and that he would sooner die with him, than deny him: yet behold the weakness and inconstancy of human nature: at the voice of a silly maid, he immediately denies his Master, repeats his denial a second and a third time, and even asserts with oaths and imprecations that he never knew the man. Sweet Jesus! what is man? Alas, O Lord, look to me, and support me by thy grace, or I also shall deny thee. The causes of Peter's fall were, *first,* A secret pride and presumption upon his own strength. *Secondly,* a neglect of the admonition of our Savior, in sleeping, when he admonished him to watch and pray. *Thirdly,* his exposing himself to the danger by running into ill company. Beware that the like causes may not produce the like effects in thee, by leading thee also to deny, and even crucify thy Lord by sin. Learn to imitate the speedy repentance of this apostle, who immediately after his fall, going out, wept bitterly; a practice which, it is said, he ever after retained, as often as he heard the cock crow.

CONSIDER, *fifthly,* how the high-priest and scribes, after having given sentence of death against our Savior, retired to take their rest, leaving him in hands that were not likely to suffer him to take any rest. Oh what a night did our Lord pass in the midst of such a rabble, who, to gratify their own cruelty, and the malice of their masters, repeated over and over again that scene of inhumanity, which they had begun whilst their masters were present, loading him with all kind of outrages and blasphemies. So that we may boldly affirm, that one half of what our Savior suffered on that night, will not be known till the day of judgment. All which insolences he not only bears in silence, but even whilst they are abusing him, he prays for them, excusing them to his Father, and offering up all his suffering in atonement for their sins. Sweet Jesus, give us the grace to imitate thee.

# 27

---

# TWENTY-SEVENTH DAY

## OUR SAVIOUR IS BROUGHT BEFORE PILATE AND HEROD

CONSIDER, *first,* how early in the morning, notwithstanding their late sitting up, the high-priest, and his fellows in iniquity, convene a more numerous assembly of the Sanhedrim, and there again put the same question to our Savior, *Whether he was the Son of God?* And receiving the same answer, confirm their former sentence. Yet as they did not think it safe for themselves, being subject to the Roman empire, to put this sentence in execution, without the consent of Pontius Pilate the governor, they determined to carry him to Pilate, and by his authority to have him crucified: a kind of execution which their malice made choice of, because it was at the same time most ignominious, as being only for vile slaves and notorious criminals; and most cruel, as being a long and lingering death, under the sharpest and most sensible torments. Come now, O Christian soul, and contemplate thy Savior, as he is hurried along the streets with his hands bound, from the house of the high-priest, to the court of Pilate, attended by the whole council, and their wicked ministers publishing aloud as they go on, that now all his impostures were laid open, his hypocrisy discovered, and himself convicted of blasphemy. Behold the giddy mob, who a little before reverenced him as a prophet, now all on a sudden Join with his enemies, following him with opprobrious shouts, insulting him all the way that he goes, and discharging a thousand kind of injuries and affronts upon him.

CONSIDER, *secondly,* and view the Judge of the living and the dead, standing with his hands bound as a criminal at the bar of a petty governor; and behold the process. The chief priests and princes of the people having delivered him up, and Pilate demanding what particulars they had to allege against him, they make no scruple of inventing fresh calumnies, viz. that he was a factious and seditious man, a traitor and rebel to the government; that he forbids tribute to be paid to Caesar, and set himself up for king of the Jews. Once more take notice of the invincible patience of thy Savior, in hearing with silence such notorious falsities as they laid to his charge; in so much that the governor was astonished that a man could be silent under such accusations, which aimed at nothing less than procuring his condemnation to the worst of deaths. However, as he plainly saw through all the disguise of the high- priest and scribes, he interpreted this silence in favor of our Savior, only hesitating a little at the word *king,* and having received full satisfaction upon that head, by being given to understand, that the kingdom of our Savior was not of this world, and therefore not dangerous to Caesar's government, he determined to set him at liberty. Admire the force of innocence, which could even move a heathen, and one of the worst of men, such as Pilate was, and assure thyself, that generally speaking, patience and silence are a thousand times better proofs of thy innocence, than returning injury for injury, and making an opprobrious and clamorous defense.

CONSIDER, *thirdly,* how Pilate being convinced of our Savior's innocence, and desirous of setting him at liberty, met with an obstinate resistance from the malicious princes and deluded people; and therefore understanding that our Savior, as being an inhabitant of Galilee, belonged to the jurisdiction of Herod, the tetrarch thereof, he from thence took occasion to rid himself of their importunity, by sending him to Herod. Accompany thy Lord, O my soul, in this new stage, and take notice of his incomparable meekness, whilst he passes through the streets, lined on all sides with an insulting multitude, and echoing with their reproaches and clamors. Herod rejoiced at his coming, in hopes to see some miracle, and therefore put a thousand questions to him; whilst the princes of the Jews, with unwearied malice, were repeating all their false accusations against him; but our Lord was still silent, nor would he satisfy the curiosity of Herod, nor do anything by which he might incline this prince to free him from that death which he so ardently desired, as being by the decrees of heaven the only means of our redemption. Blessed by all creatures be his goodness forever!

CONSIDER, *fourthly,* how Herod, provoked by our Savior's not consenting to gratify his inclinations of seeing a miracle, sought to revenge himself by treating him with mockery and scorn, exposing him to the scoffs of his guards, by ordering him to be clothed in contempt with a white garment as with a fool's coat, or perhaps as a mock king; and in this dress sent him back again to Pilate, attended in tile same manner as he came, with an insulting mob, headed by the scribes and pharisees. Stand amazed, my soul, to see the Wisdom of the eternal Father treated thus as a fool; and learn from hence, not to repine, or be solicitous about the judgment of the world.

CONSIDER, *fifthly,* how Pilate, seeing our Savior brought back again to his tribunal, contrived another way to bring him off, so as to give at the same time as little offence as might be to the high-priest, and the chief of the Jews. It was the custom of that nation on the day of their paschal solemnity, (which was celebrated that very day in memory of their delivery from the Egyptian bondage), to set at liberty one criminal, whom the people should petition for: wherefore Pilate, taking advantage of this opportunity, proposed to their choice our Savior on one hand, and Barabbas, a notorious malefactor, robber, and murderer on the other; doubting not but they would rather chose to have the innocent Lamb of God released, than that Barabbas, the worst of criminals, should escape due punishment. Ah, Pilate, what an outrageous affront dost thou here put upon the Son of God, whilst thou pretend to favor him? What must the Lord of life and immortality, the King of Heaven, stand in competition with the vilest of men, with the most notorious criminal that could be pitched upon? Must it be put to the votes of the mob, which of the two is the better man, and which the more worthy of death? O the unparalleled injury! O the unparalleled humility of my Savior! O King of glory, how low hast thou stooped to raise me up from the dunghill!

CONSIDER, *sixthly,* if it was an intolerable affront to compare our Savior with Barabbas, what idea must we frame, or what name must we give to that blind people's choice, when they preferred Barabbas to Christ, and desired that the latter might be crucified, and the former acquitted. Behold, O my soul, in this wonderful humiliation of thy Lord, how deep and dangerous was the wound of pride, which could not be cured but by so great humility: O, see if thine be yet cured. Examine thyself also, whether thou hast not often been guilty, like these blind Jews, of preferring Barabbas to thy Savior; by turning thy back on him for some petty interest, or filthy pleasure? If so, thou art more inexcusable than they, because thou knowest him to be the Lord of glory, at the same time as thou persecutes him by sin; whereas had they known him to be such, they would never have preferred a Barabbas before him.

# 28

—·—

## Twenty-eighth Day

## OUR SAVIOUR IS SCOURGED AT THE PILLAR, AND CROWNED WITH THORNS

CONSIDER, *first,* how the Jews still continuing to cry out against our Lord, and in a tumultuous manner to demand his crucifixion, Pilate contrives another way to bring about his being set at liberty, viz. by striving to satisfy their cruelty, in ordering him to be most severely scourged. O Pilate, how cruel is thy mercy! Is it thus that thou treatest him whom thou declarest innocent? Is this thy justice? But our sins, O my soul, required that the Lord of glory should be thus cruelly treated, and subjected to this ignominious punishment, to which none but common slaves or the meanest wretches are liable, and to which a Roman citizen could upon no account be condemned. Stand thou, my soul, and see in what manner this sentence is executed. Behold how the bloody soldiers lay their impious hands on this meek Lamb of God, how they strip off all his clothes, and tie him naked fast to a stone pillar; see how they discharge upon his sacred back and shoulders innumerable stripes, lashes and scourges: behold the blood come spouting forth on all sides;

see bow his body is all rent and mangled by their cruelty, and the flesh laid open to the very bones: behold his enemies all the while insulting over him, and rejoicing at his torments; whilst he, with eyes cast up towards heaven; is offering up all that he suffers for their sins, and for those of the whole world. Ah, sinners, take a serious view of your Redeemer's condition, and contemplating in his torn and mangled body, the malice of sin, learn to detest this hellish monster, which has brought on the Son of God all these sufferings.

CONSIDER, *secondly,* how these bloody ruffians by their cruel scourging having made but one wound of our Savior's body, from head to foot, loose him at last from the pillar, leaving him to put on his deaths as well as he could. Ah, Christians, have compassion now on your Savior's abandoned condition, who has no one to lend him a helping hand to bind up his gaping wounds, or stanch the blood that comes flowing from them! O, present yourselves now, and offer him what service you are able: offer at least to assist him in putting on his clothes, to cover his green wounds from the cold air. But, O how rough are these woolen clothes to his wounded back! Alas, instead of affording him any ease or comfort, they do but increase his sores, by their rubbing upon them.

CONSIDER, *thirdly,* how these merciless soldiers had scarce given our Savior a short respite after his scourging, when they were pushed on by the devil to act another scene of cruelty, such as never was heard of before or since: and that was, to make themselves a barbarous sport in crowning him a king. Therefore they drag him into the court of the

Praetorium, and assemble together the whole regiment: then violently strip him again of all his clothes, which now begin to cleave to his wounded body; set him on a bench or stool, throw about him some old ragged purple garment, twist a wreath of long, hard and sharp thorns, and press it down on his sacred head, put in his hand a reed for a scepter: then in derision, one by one, they bend their knees before him, with the scornful salutation, *Hail, King of the Jew's; they* spit in his face, buffet him, and taking the reed or cane out of his hand, strike him with it on the head, driving the thorns deeper in, whilst the blood trickles down apace from the many wounds which he receives from their points. Sweet Jesus, what shall we here say, or which shall we most admire; the malice of these ministers of Satan, or thy unparalleled charity, which made thee undergo such unheard-of reproaches and torments for ungrateful sinners? Blessed be thy goodness for ever.

CONSIDER, *fourthly,* how Pilate, hoping now that the rage and malice of the Jews would be satisfied, so as to insist no longer upon our Savior's death, after they should see with how much cruelty and contempt he had been treated, in compliance to their fury, leads him forth in the same condition, with his crown of thorns on his head, and his ragged purple on his shoulders, and from an eminence shews him to the people, saying, *Ecce homo, Behold the man.* Behold in what manner he has now been handled, cease then any longer to seek bis death. Let his body mangled from head to foot bespeak your pity. But thou, O Christian soul, *behold the man* with other kind of eyes than these hard hearted wretches; and see to what a condition thy sins and his own infinite charity have reduced him. Behold his head crowned with a wreath of sharp thorns, piercing on all sides his sacred flesh, and entering into his temples with excessive pain. Behold his face quite disfigured with blows, and quite besmeared with spittle and blood. Behold his whole-body inhumanly rent and torn with whips and scourges; and now covered with a hard ragged garment, rubbing and at each moment increasing his wounds; and then look up, and contemplate him upon his throne of glory, and see what return thou canst make him for having thus annihilated himself for love of thee. He desires no more of thee than an imitation of his patience and humility: learn then in what manner thou art to practice these lessons.

# 29

— · —

## TWENTY-NINTH DAY

### OUR SAVIOUR CARRIES HIS CROSS, AND IS NAILED TO IT

CONSIDER, *first,* how the malice of the Jews, who no way relenting at the sight of the Lamb of God bleeding for the sins of the world, but continuing still in a tumultuous manner to demand that he might be crucified, Pilate at last yields to their importunity, and against his own conscience, sentences our Savior to the death of the cross. Ah Christians, has it never been your misfortune by the like cowardice to condemn your Savior and his doctrine, and basely to renounce in the practice of your lives the maxims of the gospel, for fear of what the world will say? Has not too often a much weaker temptation than the fear of losing Caesar's friendship induced you to crucify again the Son of God? Be confounded and repent.

CONSIDER, *secondly,* that this sentence of death, how unjust soever from Pilate, yet as being most just from his eternal Father, and necessary for our salvation, was received with perfect submission, charity and silence, by our blessed Redeemer; who thereupon was immediately stripped again of his purple garment, clad with his own clothes, a heavy cross, of a length and size proportionable to the bearing of a man, laid on his wounded shoulders; and two thieves or highway robbers appointed to be his associates, and to be executed with him: to verify the prophecy, *With the wicked he was reputed,* Isai liii. Come now, devout souls, and take a view of our Lord in this his last progress or procession. A crier leads the way, publishing aloud the pretended crimes and blasphemies of this never heard of malefactor: then follow the soldiers and executioners, with ropes, hammers, nails, etc. After whom goeth, or rather creepeth along, our High-priest and Victim, all bruised and bloody, with a thief on each hand, and the cross on his shoulders, dragging it forward step by step; followed and surrounded on all sides by the priests, the scribes, and the whole mob of the people, cursing, reviling and scoffing at him; whilst the cruel executioners arc hastening him forward with their kicks and blows. Ah, Christians, now at least take pity on your Savior's sufferings, and add not to his load by your sins.

CONSIDER, *thirdly,* how our blessed Lord having for some time, with unspeakable labor and torment, carried his cross through the streets, at last falls down under its weight, unable to carry it any further. Wonder not, my soul, at this, since besides the load of the cross oppressing his weary body, wounded-in every part, and exhausted with the loss of so much blood, his heavenly Father has laid upon his shoulders another more insupportable weight, viz. that of the sins of the whole world. Ah, Christians, it is under this intolerable burthen that your Savior faints and fails down. Nor is he any way eased of this merciless load by Simon of Cyrene, who was compelled to take up the cross, but bore no part of the weight of our iniquities, all which the heavenly Father laid upon his beloved Son, to be cancelled with his blood and death. O infinite goodness of the Father! O infinite charity of the Son! to do and suffer so much for wretched man. O my soul, see thou never more be ungrateful to so loving a God.

CONSIDER, *fourthly,* how our Savior being now arrived at Mount Calvary, quite wearied and spent, the ministers of hell still persecute him with unwearied cruelty: and whereas it was the custom to give the criminals that were to die a strengthening draught of wine seasoned with myrrh, they contrived to mingle gall with the portion designed for him. After which they violently strip him of his clothes, which by this time clove fast again to his. sores, opening his wounds afresh, and exposing him naked to shame and cold in the sight of an immense multitude. Draw nigh now, my soul, and see him again bleeding for the love of thee. O see how while the cross is preparing, he falls upon his knees, and offers himself to his eternal Father a bleeding victim to appease his wrath enkindled by thy sins.

CONSIDER, fifthly how the cross lying flat on the ground, they lay our dear Redeemer stretched out upon it, who like a meek lamb makes no resistance. And first drawing his right-hand to the place designed to fix it on, they drive with their hammers a sharp gross nail through the palm, forcing its way with incredible torment through the sinews, veins, muscles and bones, of which the hand is composed, into the hard wood of the cross; in the meantime the whole body, to favor that wound and the pierced sinews, was naturally drawn towards the right side, but was not long permitted to remain so; for immediately these cruel butchers laying hold of his left arm and hand, violently drag him towards the opposite side, in order to nail that hand also to the place designed for it. Then pulling down his legs, they fastened his sacred feet in like manner with nails to the wood: and all this with such violence, that it is thought with the force of stretching and pulling they very much strained his whole body, and disjointed it in many parts, verifying the prediction of the royal prophet; *they have dug my hands and feet, they have numbered all my bones,* Ps. xxi. Ah Christians, if the contracting or piercing of a nerve or sinew; if the disjointing or displacing of a bone, though never so small, be so cruel a torture, what must we think of the torments which our Savior endured in his disjointed body! What must we think of what he suffered, when his hands and feet, where so many sinews, muscles, veins, and bones all meet, were violently bored through with gross nails! O, let us never cease to admire, adore, and love his mercy.

# 30

---·---

## THIRTIETH DAY

## OUR SAVIOR ON THE CROSS

CONSIDER, *first,* how the bloody executioners having now nailed our Savior fast to the cross, begin with ropes to raise him up in the air. O what shouts did his enemies make, when he appeared above the people's heads! with what blasphemies did they salute him! whilst his most afflicted mother, and other devout friends, stood by pierced to the heart at the sight. At length they let the foot of the cross fall with a sudden jolt into the hole prepared for it; and thus he hung suspended in the air under the most excruciating tortures, the weight of his body continually increasing the wounds in his pierced hands and feet; without any resting place for his head, but thorns; or bed for his wearied and wounded body, but the hard wood of the cross.

CONSIDER, *secondly,* the infinite charity of our Savior, and the unparalleled malice of his enemies. When in the midst of his torments, he cries out, *Father, forgive them, for they know not what they are doing:* they grin and shake their heads at him, saying, *Vah! thou that destroyest the temple of God, and rebuildest it again in three days, save now thyself if thou art the*

*Son of God, come down from the cross.* Not only the common people and soldiers, but also the chief priests and elders, unite in loading him with a thousand such like reproaches and blasphemies, which he hears and bears in patience and silence; but, O who can tell us the interior employment of his blessed soul, whilst he hangs upon the cross? his thoughts of peace towards us, his prayers for us, the anguish and dreadful agonies of the inter or part of his soul, and the inexpressible joy in the supreme part thereof, in the glory of his Father, which was to arise from that plentiful redemption, which he was then imparting to poor sinners.

CONSIDER, *thirdly,* the part that the blessed Virgin Mother bore in the sufferings of her Son; and how truly here was verified that prophecy of old Simeon, *that the sword should pierce her very soul.* O how killing a grief must have oppressed the soul of this most tender and loving of all mother's, who during the whole course of the passion of her dearest Son, whom she loved with an incomparable love, was an eyewitness to all the injuries, outrages and torments he endured. Ah blessed Lady, may we not truly say that the whips, thorns and nails, that pierced thy Son's flesh, made as deep a wound in thy virgin heart, and that nothing less than a miracle could have supported thy life under such excess of pain? But, O what a deep wound didst thou feel in thy soul, when thy dying Son recommended thee to his beloved disciple St. John, giving to thee the Son of Zebedee, in exchange for the Son of God! Blessed Virgin, we gladly acknowledge thee for our mother, an honor conferred on each of us in the person of St. John: O through all thy sufferings, remember us poor banished children of Eve, before the throne of grace. Christians, learn the admirable lessons taught you by our blessed Lady at the foot of the cross; imitate her unshaken faith and undoubted hope; perfect resignation, patience and fortitude. O learn from her to love Jesus, and detest sin, the true cause of his sufferings.

CONSIDER, *fourthly,* how all things seem now to have conspired against our dearest Lord. The thought of being forsaken by his Father, and the grief and presence of his Mother, pierce him to the heart. As for his apostles, one of them has betrayed him, another denied him, and the rest have abandoned him. His friends, and all those whom he had most favored and miraculously cured, now either join with his persecutors, or at least are ashamed of him. His enemies insult him, and triumph over him. His own body by its weight is a torment to him. But what most of all afflicts him, is the foresight of the ingratitude of Christians, the little benefit they will derive from his death and passion, and the eternal loss of so many souls redeemed by his precious blood. Ah sweet Jesus, suffer me not to be included in that unhappy number; suffer me not to be so miserable, as to join with thy enemies in crucifying thee by sin!

CONSIDER, *fifthly,* the lessons that our Savior gives us by his last words upon the cross. *First,* of perfect love and charity to his enemies, by praying for them, and pleading their excuse with his eternal Father: *Father forgive them, for they know not what they do.* O let us learn from our dying Redeemer this necessary lesson, to love and pray for those that hate and persecute us: and instead of aggravating excuse their crime and impute it to their ignorance! O how true is it of every sinner, *he knows not what he does,* otherwise he would never dare to fly in the face of infinite Majesty; he would never be so mad as to renounce heaven for a trifle, and cast himself clown the precipice that leads to hell. *Secondly,* learn the efficacy of a sincere conversion, and an humble confession of sins, in the plenary indulgence given by our dying Savior to the good thief: *Amen, I say unto thee, this day thou shalt be with me in paradise. Thirdly,* learn a filial devotion to the blessed Virgin, recommended to us as a mother by her Son, in the person of St. John, *Behold thy mother. Fourthly, l*earn the greatness of the interior anguish of thy Savior's soul from those words, *My God, my God, why hast thou forsaken me?* Alas, it was for no other reason, but that poor sinful man might not be forsaken. *Fifthly,* from that word of thy crucified Jesus, *I thirst.* It is here to be observed, that our Savior suffered two violent thirsts upon the cross; the one corporeal, proceeding from his having fasted so long, suffered so many torments, and shed so much blood; the other spiritual in his soul, by his vehement desire of our salvation. But, O cruel wretches, who would grant him nothing but vinegar to quench his corporeal thirst! and more cruel sinners, who instead of satisfying his spiritual thirst by gratitude and devotion, give him nothing but the gall of sin and vinegar of wickedness! *Sixthly,* from these words of our dying Savior, *It is consummated,* learn to rejoice that the whole work of man's redemption is now perfected; that the figure and prophecies of the law are fulfilled; and the handwriting that stood against us is now completely cancelled by the blood of our Redeemer. *Seventhly,* from

those last words of our expiring Lord, *Father into thy hands
I commend my spirit*, learn both in life and death to commit
thyself wholly to God. Happy they that study well these
lessons which their great Master teaches from the chair of his
cross.

# 31

—  ·  —

## THIRTY-FIRST DAY

## ON THE DEATH OF OUR SAVIOR

CONSIDER, first, how our Lord having spoken these last words. Father, into thy hands I commend my spirit, with a loud and strong voice, leaning down his head in perfect submission to his father's will, and perfect charity to us poor sinners, to whom in this posture he offered as it were the kiss of peace, breathed forth his pure soul, and thus ended his mortal life; which from the moment of his birth till now, had been nothing else but a series of sufferings endured for us. Hasten now my soul, and approach boldly to kiss the sacred feet of thy Redeemer, view his pale limbs, count at leisure all his wounds, and lament all thy sins, for which he suffered such exquisite torments.

CONSIDER, secondly, in the passion of our Savior, the truth of those words, which were delivered by him upon another occasion, He that humbleth himself shall be exalted: and see how our Lord, having humbled himself to the death of the cross, was even at that very time honored and exalted by his heavenly Father, and that many ways. For during the time he hung upon the cross, the sun for three whole hours withdrew his light from the world; and at his death the earth trembled, the rocks were rent asunder, and the monuments opened; the veil of the temple, which hung before the sanctuary, was rent from top to bottom: the people, touched with these wonders, went home striking their breasts; and the centurion or captain of the guards publicly professed, that this man, whom they had crucified, was truly the Son of God. Rejoice, O Christian soul, to see thy Savior's death thus honored; and learn under all events to confide in God, who will at last convert the malice of thy enemies to thy honor and advantage. Sit now down at the foot of the cross, and there at leisure,

CONSIDER, thirdly, and repeat in thy mind the multitude and variety of the sufferings which thy Savior has endured for thee, from his entrance into the garden of Gethsemani, till his expiring on the cross. View them one by one, and thou shalt see, that not one part of his sacred body (which being the most perfect, was at the same time the most sensible of pain of any that ever has been) was free from its peculiar torment. His head crowned with thorns; his face defiled with spittle, bruised, and swollen black and blue with blows; his hair and beard plucked and torn; his mouth drenched with gall and vinegar; his shoulders oppressed with the heavy weight of the cross; his hands and feet pierced with nails; his whole body exhausted with a bloody sweat, mangled and laid open with whips and scourges; his limbs wearied out, and all disjointed upon the cross. What he endured in his soul was not a jot less, but rather infinitely more painful than what be suffered in his body. Witness that mortal anguish which cast him into an agony in the garden; witness that grievous complaint on the cross, My God, my God, why hast thou forsaken me? He suffered moreover in bis reputation, by false witnesses and outrageous calumnies, which is often dearer to a man than his life: he suffered in his honor, by all manner of reproaches and affronts: be suffered in his goods, being despoiled of bis very clothes, and hanging naked upon the cross: be suffered in his friends, being forsaken by them all: not to speak of other sufferings, which are usually most sensible to flesh and blood, viz. the ingratitude of those whom he had favored with his miracles, the triumphs of his enemies, their insults over his disciples, etc. And in all these sufferings, he denied himself those comforts which he usually affords his servants under their crosses, and which have made the greatest torments of the martyrs not only tolerable, but oftentimes sweet and comfortable. But he would allow himself no other comfort, but that of doing the will of his Father, and purchasing our redemption.

CONSIDER, fourthly, who it is that suffers all this; and thou shalt find him to be the eternal Son of God, coeternal, equal, and consubstantial to his Father, the great Lord and Maker of heaven and earth; infinite in power, in wisdom, and in all perfections. But for whom does he suffer? For man, a poor wretched worm of the earth; for ungrateful sinners, traitors to his eternal Father, and to himself: for those very Jews that crucified him; for us mortals, who for the most part were never like to thank him for, or even so much as think of his sufferings. O how admirable art thou, O Lord, in all thy ways, but in none more so than in the contrivances of thy mercy! O how does the passion of our Redeemer enrich and illustrate all the attributes of God! It is here we discover his infinite goodness and charity, in thus wonderfully communicating himself to us, and laying down his life for our sakes. It is here we discover his unparalleled mercy, in taking upon himself our miseries, and enduring the stripes due to our sins. Here we behold the admirable wisdom of his providence, in opening the fountain of life to us by his death. Here we learn to fear the severity of his justice, which fell so heavy upon his only begotten Son, who had clothed himself in the semblance of a sinner, to atone for our sins. O what must the guilty themselves one day expect at his hands, if they do not prevent the terrors of his justice, by instantly embracing his mercy?

CONSIDER, fifthly, in the sufferings of thy Savior, the infinite malice, the unparalleled heinousness of mortal sin, which could not be cancelled but by the blood of the Son of God. This is the chief lesson which thy Savior desires to teach thee, from the chair of the cross; thou canst not please him better than by studying it well. O never then be so ungrateful as to crucify him again by mortal sin. O suffer not that monster to live in thee, for the destroying of which, Christ himself would die.

# RULES OF A CHRISTIAN LIFE

## TO BE OBSERVED BY SWITCH AS DESIRE TO SECURE TO THEMSELVES A HAPPY ETERNITY

1. SETTLE in thy soul a firm resolution, on no account whatever to consent to mortal sin. This resolution is the very foundation of a virtuous life: whosoever is not arrived thus far, has not yet begun to serve God. Without this resolution, it is in vain for anyone to flatter himself with the hopes of living holily or dying happily.

2. In order to enable thyself to keep this resolution, be diligent in Hying all dangerous occasions, such as bad company, lewd or profane books, immodest plays, etc. *For he that loves danger, shall perish in it,* Eccl. ii. 27.

3. Watch every motion of thy heart and resist the first impressions of evil; keep a strict guard upon thy senses and imagination, that the enemy may not surprise thy soul by these avenues. Contemn not

small faults, lest by degrees, thou fall into greater.

4. Fly an idle life, as the mother of all mischief, and take it for a certain truth, that indolence will never bring a Christian to heaven.

5. Never omit, upon any account, thy morning and evening prayers. Remember in the morning to present to God the first fruits of the day, by giving him thy first thoughts: make an offering to him of all the actions of the day; and renew this oblation at the beginning of everything thou dost, *Whether you eat or drink,* says St. Paul, 1 Cor. x. 31. *or whatever else you do, do all for the glory of God.*

6. In thy evening prayers make a strict examination of conscience, calling thyself to an account how thou hast passed the day; and whatever sins thou discoverest, labor to wash them away by penitential tears before thou layest thyself down to sleep: for who knows but that night may be thy last. In going to bed think on the grave; compose thyself to rest in the arms of thy God; and if thou wake in the night, raise thy thoughts to him, who always watches over thee.

7. Besides morning and evening devotions, set apart sometime in the day for prayer, particularly *mental,* by an interior Conversation of thy soul with God, her only sovereign good. In the midst of all thy employments, keep thyself as much as

possible in the presence of God, and frequently aspire to him by short ejaculations. Read often spiritual books, as letters or messages sent thee from heaven. And if thy circumstances permit, assist daily at the sacrifice of the mass.

8. Frequent the sacraments at least once a month and take special care to prepare thyself to receive them worthily.

Have a great devotion to the passion of Christ, and often meditate upon his sufferings.

Be particularly devout to his blessed mother; take her for thy mother and seek upon all occasions her protection and prayers; but learn withal to imitate her virtues.

Study to find out thy predominant passion, and labor with all thy power to root it up.

Let not a day pass without offering to God some acts of contrition for past sins: and strive to nourish in thy soul a penitential spirit.

Beware of self-love as thy greatest enemy; and often use violence to thyself by self-denials and mortifications: for, remember the kingdom of heaven is not to be taken but by violnce, St. Matt. xi. 12.

Give alms according to thy ability for *judgment without mercy, to him that has not shewed mercy fit.* James ii. 13. Set a great value upon spiritual alms-deeds, by endeavoring to reclaim unhappy sinners; and for that end daily bewail their-misery in the sight of God.

Be exact in all the duties of thy calling, as being to give an account one day to that great blaster, who has allotted to each one of us our respective station in his family.

*Remember* always thy *last things, and thou shalt never sin,* Eccl. vii.